# SOUP

## 100 SENSATIONAL SOUP RECIPES

# SOUP!

## GENEVIEVE TAYLOR

**100 SENSATIONAL SOUP RECIPES**

First published in Great Britain in 2012
by **Absolute Press**, an imprint of
Bloomsbury Publishing Plc

Scarborough House
29 James Street West
Bath BA1 2BT
**Phone** 44 (0) 1225 316013
**Fax** 44 (0) 1225 445836
**E-mail** info@absolutepress.co.uk
**Website** www.absolutepress.co.uk

Text copyright
© Genevieve Taylor, 2012
This edition copyright
© Absolute Press, 2012
Photography copyright © Mike Cooper

**Publisher** Jon Croft
**Commissioning Editor** Meg Avent
**Art Director** Matt Inwood
**Design** Matt Inwood
and Claire Siggery
**Editor** Anne Sheasby
**Photography** Mike Cooper
**Food Styling** Genevieve Taylor

**ISBN: 9781906650704**

Printed and bound in China on
behalf of Latitude Press

**Bloomsbury Publishing Plc**
50 Bedford Square
London WC1B 3DP
www.bloomsbury.com

**A note about the text**
This book was set using ITC Century
and Serifa. The first Century typeface
was cut in 1894. In 1975, an updated
family of Century typefaces was
designed by Tony Stan for ITC.
The Serifa font was designed by
Adrian Frutiger in 1978.

**Thanks**
I have really loved writing *Soup!*, not
least because I spent so much time in
my kitchen, testing and tasting my way
through these recipes. My freezer is
now nicely stocked with enough soup
to see me through winter! So a big
thanks go to my publisher, Absolute
Press, for honoring me with the job.
The team at Absolute Press did so much
more than simply ask me to write it.
Thanks should go to Jon Croft,
publisher and grande fromage, for
trusting me to deliver once again.
And to Matt Inwood and Claire Siggery
for their beautiful design work, and to
Matt as well for his general support
and encouragement throughout. Anne
Sheasby, my editor, gets a big thank you
for her fastidious reading and correcting
of my manuscript. It all flows so
much better for her thorough tweaks.
Thanks, once again, to the super-
talented Mike Cooper, whose
gorgeous photography you see
throughout this book. Working with
Mike is always an easy pleasure.
And last, but very much not least,
thanks to my wonderful family, whose
support, love and encouragement keep
me going even when the deadlines are
looming. Rob, Izaac and Eve – I love
you more than all the soup in all the
world. One day, kids, you might get
over your soup phobia and who
knows, maybe you will even grow to
like it?  And Mum, thanks for giving me
inspiration for many of these recipes.
I remember you cooking lots of
wonderful soups, and many other
delicious things, when I was young.
But one day you must tell me how
you got me to eat it!

# INTRO

**Soup has to be one of the most versatile and diverse of all dishes and for that I applaud it – few things are more pleasurable to eat than a bowl of homemade soup. Warming in winter, cooling in summer, there is always a perfect bowlful of soup for every occasion.**

The appeal of soup is gloriously multi-faceted. Generally very easy to make and often quick too, a good many of the recipes in this book can be on the table with little effort and time involved. A real bonus when hunger pangs strike. Soups are also a great way to use up leftovers, appealing to the need we all have to be economical and frugal from time to time. No matter how bare your larder may be, it is usually possible to find a few bits and pieces with which to make a delicious soup. Soups are also a wonderful way to encompass seasonality, a way of eating that is, quite rightly, gaining more and more importance to the home cook. Making soups is a hugely satisfying way to use gluts of produce from your own garden or from the supermarket or veg shop. And of course, with all those vegetables, many soups pack a nutritious punch that is hard to beat.

I think one of the nicest ways to serve soup is with a few embellishments for scattering over at the end. A little garnish of something tasty will elevate your soup to the next level. It is not just about making it look pretty – although we eat with our eyes as well as our mouths, so to my mind presentation is vital. It's also about creating interest and variety with a contrast of textures and taste sensations as you eat. So, what could be more delicious than a smooth sweet potato soup garnished with crisp chilli-spiced beef sprinkles, or a chilled creamy avocado soup served with hot buttered garlic prawns scattered over?

With all these things going for it, it's not hard to see why soup is truly a global food, with every country in the world having their own specialities. I hope this book offers you a wealth of ideas for every occasion, and that as well as using my recipes, you are inspired to try some of your own creations. So, celebrate soup – the possibilities are almost endless!

## Happy cooking.

**Genevieve Taylor**
**Bristol, December 2011**

### A note on texture

Soups can be thick and wholesome, or thin and brothy, velvety smooth or rustically lumpy – and an infinite variety of combinations in between. The texture of food, I think, is a rather personal thing and I would urge you not to follow my rules to the letter. I tend to like soup thickish, with the exception of the oriental types hot with chilli, but if you prefer yours thinner, simply add more stock, water or milk until it's perfect for you.

In the soups made with milk, you will see that I often use a little flour as a thickener. The flour seems to bind the whole thing together cohesively, stabilizing it and making it less likely to curdle. However, if you have a gluten allergy or simply prefer not to use flour, then it can be left out.

Different textures can also be achieved with different tools. A potato masher in a pan of bean soup will break up a few beans and thicken the sauce. A stick blender placed into a pan of soup will do the same job but more effectively – if you want a smoothish soup with some texture, this is the best and most convenient option. But if it's velvet-smoothness you require – and there are definitely some soups that need this – then a blender, possibly even followed by a sieve as you pour the soup back into the pan, is the way to go.

### A note on stocks

Stock cubes and ready-made stocks, good quality ones, have nothing to be ashamed of. I use them often for instant flavour and ultimate convenience. But there is no denying that homemade stock is far superior and it pays to know when it's worth the extra effort to make your own. As a rule of thumb, I find that the thin and brothy soups benefit hugely from homemade stock. Chicken stock, made slowly and with care, will add an unctuousness that can never be replicated with a stock cube. Conversely, thicker soups, or those fragrant with spices, are more forgiving of the quick ready-made option.

In this book there are some basic recipes for stock (see below for page references) but it's worth knowing what herbs and bits and bobs are good to add. I never peel my onions but merely chop them roughly – the skin will add a wonderful deep colour. Mushrooms, or even mushroom stalks leftover from another recipe, also add colour and depth, likewise trimmings from asparagus or parsley stalks. Anything starchy, like potatoes, parsnips or squash are not good for stock as they will cloud and thicken it. Black peppercorns, left whole, are essential, but I would never add salt as the liquid reduces quite considerably as you cook, concentrating the flavours, so it would be very easy to over-salt.

Stock freezes really well so it's a good idea to make a double batch and freeze what you don't use. It's useful to write the volume of stock onto the bag as well as the name so you know how much you are defrosting. See page 8 for more tips on freezing.

Finally, and I think most importantly, stock should never be boiled and should only be simmered over a low heat. If you boil meat stock, you emulsify the fat and the resulting stock will always be cloudy and murky.

### Basic vegetable stock (page 15)

Vegetable stock can be made with all sorts of different bits and pieces of veg and is a great way of using up surplus stock from your fridge or veg drawer. The recipe on page 15 is just a guide – don't be constrained by it, but don't be tempted to add any starchy veg to your stock or it will cloud and thicken it. When I'm cooking, I often save fresh herb stems or trimmings from asparagus or mushrooms to add to the stock-pot as it seems like a criminal waste of a flavour opportunity to throw them away. Some fresh herbs, such as rosemary and sage, are rather strong and I would advise not adding too much of these as they can become a little overpowering.

**7 SOUP! INTRODUCTION**

### Basic chicken stock (page 12)

Chicken stock is probably the one I make most frequently at home, normally from the leftovers of a roast chicken. Occasionally, when it's paramount to get a really clean chicken flavour, I will make the stock using uncooked chicken wings. In either case, I always use a free-range or organic bird. Quite apart from the welfare considerations, for the cook they simply yield far more flavour. Free-range birds are generally a couple of weeks older at slaughter than their non-free-range counterparts, and organic birds are usually over twice the age. That maturity, plus the higher welfare, the freedom to exercise and a better diet, mean the bones and muscles are more developed and so have more flavour.

I always make my chicken stock in a low oven. I find it convenient as I can leave it all day or all night, unattended, and by cooking it very slowly, the resulting stock is as clear as a bell.

### Basic beef or lamb stock (page 26)

With red meat stocks, a bit more time and attention is needed and they are just a bit more of a faff to make. For that reason, I tend to revert to using good quality ready-made versions more often than with the simpler stocks. But if you have time to make your own, the rewards in the taste department will be great. With beef or lamb stock, I like to brown the bones in a hot oven first, as this produces a richer and darker stock.

### Basic fish stock (page 56)

There are two cardinal rules for making a fish stock. Firstly, you mustn't cook it for too long or it will turn cloudy and the bones will impart a bitter taste. Secondly, stay clear of using oily fish, such a mackerel, herring or salmon, otherwise the stock will have an unpleasant oily taste. Shells from prawns make an excellent addition and will give you a rich colour and depth of flavour.

### A note on freezing soups

Many soups freeze brilliantly meaning that they are an excellent choice for batch-cooking and freezing in portions. What could be nicer on a chilly day than finding some hearty soup in the freezer for lunch?

I tend to freeze food in freezer bags, as I find I can pack them more neatly and compactly than if I used boxes. The most important thing, a bit boring I know, is to make sure you label the bag or box with both the contents and date. Freeze soups for up to 3 months – after that, the flavour can start to deteriorate.

To defrost, leave the frozen soup in the fridge overnight, then reheat thoroughly in a saucepan the next day. Alternatively, defrost the soup in the microwave using the defrost setting, then transfer it to a saucepan and reheat thoroughly until piping hot. I find that soup that has been frozen is often a bit too thick on reheating. If this is the case, simply add a little more water, stock or milk to thin it to the desired consistency.

### A note on butter

In the majority of recipes that use butter, you will note that I specify using the unsalted type. Not just a cheffy fad, the reason for this is pure science. Unsalted butter has a higher burning point than salted butter, and for the cook, this means that unsalted butter is much less likely to burn than salted butter and so is the best type to use when doing any sort of frying. A little splash of oil, either olive or any other vegetable oil, added as the butter melts will reduce the chances of burning even more.

I tend to only buy unsalted butter and use it for all my baking, frying and eating. But as a real treat, sometimes I take a hunk of buttered bread – so perfect for dunking in soup – and sprinkle over a little flaky sea salt to give a gorgeous saline crunch as I bite into it.

INTRO

### A note on spices
Just like us all, dried spices do age over time, their intensity deteriorating as the months roll by. Many people will have jars of spices lined up in a cupboard that have happily been gathering dust for years. One word of advice – chuck them out and start again. Spices that have a vibrant colour, like turmeric and paprika, should still have a vivid hue; spices that are characterized by a strong pungent flavour, like cumin, should still hit your nostrils as soon as you lift the lid of the jar. If they smell a bit musty and dusty, the chances are they will be verging on the elderly and won't give you their best flavour. I would really only keep whole spices for a year at most, ground ones even less than that. The one exception to this rule seems to be whole nutmeg – I have some that are still in their shells and, at nearly a decade old, are tasting as good as ever.

It pays to buy spices whole and grind them yourself as you will get a much more intense aroma. In some recipes, you will see I call for 'dry-frying' the spices before you use them. This is particularly true for cumin which really benefits from a little heat to wake it up.

### A note on preparation and cooking times
To calculate preparation and cooking times in this book, I have followed a set of my own 'rules' to try and ensure consistency. These are very simple and are aimed at giving you an idea of how long it should take to get your soup to the table. Preparation time includes all the steps up until the liquid goes in the soup, after which time it becomes cooking time. So, soups with a long prep time and short cooking time will mean that something, like roasting of vegetables, has to happen before it reaches a liquid stage. And in some soups, the prep time is short and the cooking time is lengthy, like in the soups with dried pulses. Talking of dried pulses, it can be tricky to give accurate timings for their cooking – my chickpeas may cook in half the time of your chickpeas. Many factors, such as age and dryness, will affect their cooking times hugely.

Therefore, you may find you need to add more water or stock than I indicate – just keep a bit of a watchful eye on them from time to time during cooking.

### A note on serving quantities
All the recipes in this book are listed as serving 4–6 people. Judging appetite is always a tricky thing and it goes without saying if you are serving your soup as a starter, you will need less per person than if it is to be the main part of your meal. So be guided by your greed. I hope these recipes verge on the generous in terms of portion size, as that is the way I like to feed people!

# COMFORTING

When we think of soup we tend to think of bowls of steaming comfort, and nothing shouts 'home' more than a pan of soup simmering on the hob. These are soups to feed the soul and nourish the body – it is no surprise that chicken soup is thought of as the perfect thing for recuperating after an illness. And it is not an exaggeration to say that a bowl of homemade soup can simply make you feel better about yourself and the world around you.

# Butter Bean, Chorizo and Parsley Soup

I make this soup with cans of ready-cooked butter beans, which gives you a meal on the table far quicker than if you used dried beans. I find that cooking butter beans from dry can be a bit hit and miss – their skins seem to fall off and some go mushy and overcooked whilst others stay hard.

**Serves 4–6 | Takes 10 minutes to make, 20 minutes to cook**

**1 tbsp olive oil**
**1 large red onion, finely chopped**
**150g piece of chorizo, finely sliced**
**3 cloves garlic, crushed**
**2 x 400g cans butter beans, drained and rinsed**
**1 litre chicken stock (opposite)**
**large bunch of fresh flat-leaf parsley, roughly chopped**
**salt and freshly ground black pepper**

Heat the oil in a large saucepan, add the onion and fry over a medium-high heat for about 5 minutes or until it softens and begins to caramelise.

Add the chorizo and continue to fry gently for another 5 minutes or so until the sausage begins to release its wonderful smoky oils.

Stir through the garlic and drained butter beans, then pour in the stock. Season with a little salt and freshly ground black pepper. Bring up to the boil, then lower the heat and simmer gently, uncovered, for 10 minutes.

Stir through the parsley and simmer for a further minute. Taste to check the seasoning, adding a little more salt and black pepper, if necessary, then serve.

**Not suitable for freezing.**

**Basic Chicken Stock**

**1 roast chicken carcass, broken into pieces or 500g raw chicken wings (preferably free-range or organic)**
**2 onions, unpeeled and cut into quarters**
**2 fat carrots, cut into chunks**
**2 sticks celery, cut into chunks**
**1 tsp black peppercorns**
**handful of fresh parsley stalks**
**2 bay leaves**

Preheat the oven to 140°C/gas 1. Add everything to a stock-pot and cover generously with cold water – you will need around 1.5–2 litres cold water. Bring slowly up to the boil, then cover tightly with a lid or with a tight-fitting piece of foil. Transfer the stock-pot to the oven and cook for 6–8 hours. Alternatively, cook, uncovered, on the hob as slowly as possible and for at least 4 hours. Strain, then use as required, or cool and store in a covered container in the fridge and use within 3 days. The stock can be frozen for up to 3 months (see page 8 for more guidance on freezing).

# Ham and Split Pea Soup

This is just the kind of delicious hearty soup you need to warm you up from the inside on a cold winter's day. It's a great way of using up leftover bits of ham or gammon from roast joints, making it really economical as well. If your ham was cooked on the bone, add the bone to the soup whilst it is simmering as this will really enhance the flavour.

**Serves 4–6 | Takes 15 minutes to make, 40 minutes to cook**

**1 tbsp vegetable oil**
**3 sticks celery, diced**
**2 carrots, diced**
**1 large onion, finely chopped**
**300g dried split peas (green or yellow)**
**2 bay leaves**
**250g piece of cooked ham, shredded**
**salt and freshly ground black pepper**

Heat the oil in a large saucepan and gently sweat the celery, carrots and onion until they are just beginning to soften. Add the split peas and bay leaves and season with plenty of freshly ground black pepper but no salt at this stage as it will toughen up the peas. If you have a ham bone, add this too for extra flavour.

Pour over 1.5 litres cold water and bring up to the boil. Lower the heat and simmer steadily, uncovered, for about 40 minutes or until the peas are soft and cooked through but not completely disintegrating. If the soup is becoming a little thick, add a splash more water.

Add the ham and cook for a further few minutes to warm through. Taste to check the seasoning, adding a little salt, if necessary. Serve hot with plenty of buttered crusty bread.

**Not suitable for freezing.**

# Cuban Black Bean and Sour Cream Soup

**Pure comfort in a bowl, this soup looks dark and inviting. A generous dollop of sour cream on top not only looks pretty but adds a vital sharpness to balance the rich meaty beans. If you are a vegetarian, leave out the bacon but add a spoonful of Spanish smoked paprika for essential smoky flavour.**

**Serves 4–6 | Takes 15 minutes to make, plus overnight soaking of the beans, 1 hour to cook**

**350g dried black beans, soaked overnight in cold water, drained and rinsed**
**2 tbsp vegetable oil**
**4 rashers smoked streaky bacon, cut into 1cm strips or dice**
**1 large onion, finely chopped**
**2 sticks celery, finely chopped**
**2 carrots, finely chopped**
**1 red pepper, deseeded and finely chopped**
**1 tsp dark soft brown (muscovado) sugar**
**1 tsp cayenne pepper**
**1.5–2 litres chicken (page 12) or vegetable stock (opposite)**
**salt and freshly ground black pepper**
**sour cream, a few fresh coriander leaves and lime wedges for squeezing, to serve**

Heat the oil in a large saucepan and gently sweat the bacon with the onion, celery, carrots and red pepper for 5 minutes.

Add the drained beans, sugar and cayenne pepper and then pour over the stock. Bring up to the boil and boil rapidly for 10 minutes. Turn the heat down to a simmer and carry on cooking, uncovered, until the beans are soft and tender – this should take around 1 hour.

I like this soup thick and almost stew-like, so towards the end of cooking, mash up some of the beans with a wooden spoon or potato masher. You may need to add a little extra water or stock if you want a looser texture.

Season to taste with salt and freshly ground black pepper. Serve each portion with a dollop of sour cream, a few coriander leaves and a lime wedge to squeeze over just before you dig in.

**Not suitable for freezing.**

**Basic Vegetable Stock**
**2 large onions, finely sliced, plus the skins**
**3 carrots, sliced**
**3 sticks celery, sliced**
**3 cloves garlic, bruised but unpeeled**
**2–3 bay leaves, plus a generous handful of other fresh herbs, such as parsley, thyme, sage and tarragon (stalks and all)**
**1 tsp black peppercorns**

Add all the ingredients to a large saucepan and cover with 2 litres cold water. Bring slowly up to the boil, then reduce the heat to a steady simmer and cook, uncovered, for 1 hour. Strain, then use as required, or cool and store in a covered container in the fridge and use within 3 days. The stock can be frozen for up to 3 months (see page 8 for more guidance on freezing).

# Bessara

This soup hails from North Africa, where it is made with either split peas or dried fava beans. Split peas are easier to find over here so I tend to make it with these. Some bessara recipes call for you to cook the peas separately before adding them to the soup. Trying to cut a few corners one day, I tried to make it all in one pan and, to my mind, it worked just as well and saved on an all important washing-up step.

**Serves 4–6 | Takes 15 minutes to make, 50 minutes to cook**

**2 tbsp cumin seeds**
**2 tbsp olive oil**
**1 large onion, finely sliced**
**3 cloves garlic, crushed**
**1 tsp dried chilli flakes**
**350g dried split peas (green or yellow)**
**1.75 litres vegetable stock**
**salt and freshly ground black pepper**
**extra virgin olive oil and a loose handful of roughly chopped fresh coriander leaves, to serve**

In a large, heavy-based saucepan, dry-fry the cumin seeds for a minute or two, taking care not to burn them. As soon as you smell their nutty aroma wafting up from the pan, tip them into a pestle and mortar and coarsely grind.

Add the olive oil to the pan, along with the onion and sweat for around 10 minutes or until softened and lightly caramelised. Add the garlic, dried chilli and half of the crushed cumin and fry for a further minute. Reserve the remaining cumin – it gets added at the end for a fresh boost of spice flavour.

Tip in the split peas and pour over the stock. Bring up to the boil, then reduce the heat and simmer steadily, uncovered, for 50 minutes or so until the peas are completely soft.

Purée the soup until it is smooth, either using a stick blender in the pan, or carefully transfer the soup to a blender and purée, adding a little water if it is too thick, then return to the pan and reheat gently until hot.

Add the remaining cumin and season to taste with salt and freshly ground black pepper. Serve in deep bowls with a drizzle of extra virgin olive oil and a little chopped coriander leaf.

**This soup freezes very well – freeze for up to 3 months. Defrost thoroughly, then reheat gently until piping hot. See page 8 for more guidance on this.**

# Cauliflower Cheese Soup with Wholegrain Mustard

**Cauliflower and cheese is such a classic combination and the mustard gives it just a hint of peppery heat that is delicious. I like to serve this with plenty of thick-cut granary toast, the wholesomeness of which seems to strike the right balance against the richness of the soup.**

**Serves 4–6 | Takes 10 minutes to make, 20 minutes to cook**

**50g unsalted butter**
**1 onion, chopped**
**1 large cauliflower, leaves and main stalk discarded, florets roughly chopped**
**1 large potato, cut into 1cm cubes**
**500ml milk**
**500ml vegetable stock**
**1 bay leaf**
**150g mature Cheddar cheese, grated**
**1–2 tbsp wholegrain mustard**
**salt and freshly ground black pepper**

In a large saucepan, melt the butter over a low heat and gently sweat the onion for 10 minutes or so until soft and translucent.

Add the cauliflower and potato, pour in the milk and stock and bring up to a steady simmer. Add the bay leaf and season with a little salt and freshly ground black pepper. Simmer, uncovered, for 15–20 minutes or until the cauliflower and potatoes are really soft.

Fish out the bay leaf and discard, then carefully transfer the soup to a blender and purée until really smooth – do this in batches, if necessary. Return to the pan, add the cheese, then add the mustard to taste, stirring thoroughly to mix, and bring back to a gentle simmer. Do not boil as the cheese may separate into a slightly grainy texture, which doesn't ruin the taste but does look a little unsightly.

Taste to check the seasoning and add a little more salt and black pepper, if necessary. Serve hot with plenty of bread.

**This soup freezes really well – freeze for up to 3 months. Defrost thoroughly, then reheat gently until piping hot. See page 8 for more guidance on this.**

# Puy Lentil and Pancetta Soup with Parmesan Toasts

**Puy lentils hold their shape when cooked, unlike red lentils, so they give this wholesome soup a rustic nutty texture. The Parmesan toasts add a really savoury crunch and make the dish feel a little bit special.**

**Serves 4–6 | Takes 15 minutes to make, 40 minutes to cook**

**2 tbsp olive oil**
**2 sticks celery, finely chopped**
**1 large onion, finely chopped**
**1 carrot, finely chopped**
**150g pancetta (preferably smoked), diced**
**2 cloves garlic, crushed**
**180g Puy lentils**
**1.5 litres vegetable or chicken stock**
**4 sprigs of fresh oregano or marjoram, leaves picked and roughly chopped**
**handful of fresh flat-leaf parsley, roughly chopped**
**salt and freshly ground black pepper**

**For the Parmesan toasts**
**$\frac{1}{2}$ baguette, cut into thin slices**
**1 clove garlic, bruised and cut in half**
**2 tbsp olive oil**
**50g fresh Parmesan cheese, finely grated**

Heat the oil in a large, heavy-based saucepan and gently sweat the celery, onion, carrot and pancetta until the vegetables are starting to soften. Add the garlic and cook for a further minute or so.

Stir through the lentils and pour over the stock. Bring up to the boil, then lower the heat a little and simmer steadily, uncovered, for around 35–40 minutes or until the lentils are tender. Towards the end of cooking, you may need to add a splash of water if the soup is getting a little thick.

Remove from the heat, stir through the chopped herbs and season to taste with salt and freshly ground black pepper.

When the soup is nearly ready, make the Parmesan toasts. Toast the baguette slices under the grill until crisp and golden on one side. Rub the bruised garlic over the untoasted sides and drizzle over the oil. Sprinkle the Parmesan cheese on top and grind over a little black pepper. Return to the grill until the cheese has melted and the bread has crisped at the edges.

Serve the hot soup with the Parmesan toasts floating on top.

**This soup freezes really well (without the Parmesan toasts) – freeze for up to 3 months. Defrost thoroughly, then reheat gently until piping hot. See page 8 for more guidance on this. Parmesan toasts not suitable for freezing, so make these just before serving.**

# Moroccan Roast Tomato, Red Pepper and Chickpea Soup

**This is an easy, colourful soup to make and roasting the vegetables really enriches the flavour. You could ring the changes and substitute some of the peppers for other Mediterranean-style vegetables like courgettes and aubergines.**

**Serves 4–6 | Takes 30 minutes to make, 10 minutes to cook**

**6 medium tomatoes, cut into chunks**
**3 red peppers, deseeded and cut into bite-sized pieces**
**4 cloves garlic, roughly chopped**
**4 tbsp olive oil**
**1 tbsp cumin seeds**
**1 tbsp coriander seeds**
**400g can chickpeas, drained and rinsed**
**750ml vegetable stock**
**salt and freshly ground black pepper**
**handful of fresh coriander leaves, roughly chopped, and extra virgin olive oil, to garnish**

Preheat the oven to 190°C/gas 5.

In a large roasting tin, toss the tomatoes, peppers and garlic in the olive oil and spices. Season with a little salt and freshly ground black pepper and roast in the oven for 30 minutes or until soft and slightly crisp at the edges.

Remove from the oven, add the drained chickpeas and stir well. Carefully tip half of the roasted vegetable and chickpea mixture into a blender, add all of the stock and purée until smooth.

Pour into a saucepan and add the remaining roasted vegetable and chickpea mixture. Bring up to a gentle simmer and taste to check the seasoning, adding a little more salt and black pepper, if necessary.

Serve garnished with a little chopped coriander and a generous drizzle of extra virgin olive oil.

**This soup does freeze (but the chunks of pepper tend to lose a little of their texture) – freeze for up to 3 months. Defrost thoroughly, then reheat gently until piping hot. See page 8 for more guidance on this.**

# Bean and Pork Soup

**This is a hearty main meal soup, perfect for a chilly autumn evening. The trick is to fry the pork over as high a heat as you dare to get a really dark caramelised crust which will add bags of flavour to the finished soup.**

**Serves 4–6 | Takes 20 minutes to make, plus overnight soaking of the beans and marinating of the pork, $1^{1}/_{4}$ hours to cook**

**250g dried pinto beans, soaked overnight in cold water, drained and rinsed**

**To marinate the pork**
**2 tbsp dark soft brown sugar**
**2 tbsp red wine vinegar**
**1 tbsp vegetable oil**
**3 cloves garlic, crushed**
**2 tsp cumin seeds, roughly ground**
**1 tsp dried chilli flakes**
**4 thick slices boneless belly pork, cut into bite-sized chunks**
**salt and freshly ground black pepper**

**For the soup**
**1 large red onion, finely chopped**
**2 medium-hot long fresh red chillies, deseeded and finely chopped**
**400g can chopped tomatoes**
**1.5 litres chicken stock**
**2 bay leaves**
**2 tsp dried thyme**

**For the guacamole**
**2 ripe avocados**
**1–2 cloves garlic, crushed**
**1 tbsp crème fraîche or sour cream**
**juice of $^{1}/_{2}$ lime**

Firstly marinate the pork. In a non-metallic bowl, mix together all the ingredients for the marinade, seasoning it with salt and freshly ground black pepper, then add the pork, tossing to coat it all over. Cover with cling film and marinate in the fridge for at least 3 hours, preferably overnight. I tend to marinate the pork when I put the beans on to soak – that way I know it gets plenty of time to absorb lots of lovely flavour.

When you are ready to cook the soup, heat a large, heavy-based saucepan until it is hot. Fry the pork in batches until deeply caramelised all over – don't overcrowd the pan otherwise the pork will sweat rather than fry – setting each batch aside on a plate as it is done. Be brave with this step as the caramelisation will add an intense flavour to the finished soup – you can even let it burn ever so slightly in places.

Once all the pork has been browned, return it all to the pan along with the onion, chillies and drained beans. Pour in the tomatoes and stock, add the bay leaves and thyme and bring up to the boil, then boil rapidly for 10 minutes. Lower the heat to a steady simmer and continue to cook, uncovered, until the beans are really tender – this will take around $1–1^{1}/_{4}$ hours. Add a splash more water if the soup is looking a little dry.

Whilst the soup is cooking, make the guacamole. Halve and stone the avocados, then scoop out the flesh into a small bowl (discarding the peel) and mash with a fork. Stir through the garlic, crème fraîche and lime juice. Season to taste with salt and freshly ground black pepper, cover and chill in the fridge until needed.

When the soup is cooked, taste to check the seasoning, adding salt and freshly ground black pepper, if necessary. Serve the hot soup with a good dollop of guacamole on top of each portion.

**This soup freezes well, but the guacamole does not. Freeze the soup for up to 3 months. Defrost thoroughly, then reheat gently until piping hot. See page 8 for more guidance on this. Guacamole not suitable for freezing, so make this just before serving.**

# Potato, Sweetcorn and Bacon Chowder

In terms of food, 'comfort' to me often translates to mean creamy and rich, something to treat myself to. When you need a hug-in-a-bowl, this soup really fits the bill – salty, savoury and creamy with just a hint of wine – delicious! I would even go as far as to suggest you add a swirl of single cream at the end.

**Serves 4–6 | Takes 15 minutes to make, 20 minutes to cook**

**25g unsalted butter**
**1 large onion, chopped**
**6 rashers smoked streaky bacon, diced**
**2 cloves garlic, chopped**
**2 large potatoes (about 400g in total), cut into 1cm cubes**
**2 carrots, diced**
**150g sweetcorn kernels (canned or frozen)**
**1 tsp dried thyme**
**500ml milk**
**500ml vegetable stock**
**200ml dry white wine**
**salt and freshly ground black pepper**
**single cream (optional) and a little roughly chopped fresh flat-leaf parsley, to serve**

Melt the butter in a large saucepan over a low heat and sweat the onion with the bacon for about 5 minutes or until the onion is slightly softened. Add the garlic and cook for a further minute before adding the potatoes, carrots and sweetcorn, stirring well to mix.

Stir through the thyme and pour in the milk, stock and wine and season with a little salt and plenty of freshly ground black pepper. Bring up to the boil, then lower the heat a little and simmer steadily, uncovered, for about 20 minutes or until the vegetables are soft and tender. Towards the end of cooking, I like to use a potato masher to lightly break up some of the vegetables and thicken the soup slightly.

Serve in generous bowls with a swirl of cream, if you like, and a sprinkling of parsley.

**This soup freezes well (although the vegetables may become a bit more broken up on reheating) – freeze for up to 3 months. Defrost thoroughly, then reheat gently until piping hot. See page 8 for more guidance on this.**

# Chicken, Wild Rice and Pea Soup

**This calming and soothing broth-style soup is given a lovely lift with a little fresh coriander at the end. If you don't like coriander, try some parsley or chives instead – a sprinkle of something fragrant and green is often a great way to inject a bit of freshness into a dish just before you serve it.**

**Serves 4–6 | Takes 20 minutes to make, 45 minutes to cook**

**2 tbsp olive oil**
**4 chicken thighs, bone in and skin on**
**2 onions, chopped**
**2–3 cloves garlic, sliced**
**1 litre chicken stock**
**150g wild rice**
**150g frozen peas (no need to defrost)**
**handful of roughly chopped fresh coriander (or other herbs like parsley or chives)**
**salt and freshly ground black pepper**

Heat the oil in a heavy-based saucepan until it is smoking hot – I find a large cast iron casserole to be the best thing for the job. Once the oil is hot, fry the chicken, skin-side down, until golden brown, then turn over and fry the other side until golden brown. It's important to get some good colour on the chicken, as it will add bags of flavour to the finished soup.

Once the chicken is golden all over, lower the heat and add the onions. Continue to cook until the onions are lightly caramelised, then stir through the garlic. Pour in the stock, add the rice and season with a little salt and freshly ground black pepper. Bring up to a simmer and cook steadily, uncovered, for about 45 minutes or until the rice is tender and the chicken is cooked through.

Stir through the frozen peas and simmer for another few minutes until just cooked. Remove from the heat, stir through the herbs and taste to check the seasoning, adding a little more salt and black pepper, if necessary.

Serve the soup in bowls with a piece of chicken on top of each portion. Alternatively, remove the meat from the chicken thighs (discarding the bones) and stir through the soup.

**This soup freezes well – freeze for up to 3 months. Defrost thoroughly, then reheat gently until piping hot. See page 8 for more guidance on this.**

# Tomato and Red Lentil Soup

This easy, cheap and filling soup reminds of me of my student days when I used to make a huge vat of it, enough to last all week. These days I like a little more variety in my culinary life, but I often still make it in double quantities as it freezes very well, so it makes an excellent standby to have on hand when you haven't got the time or inclination to cook.

**Serves 4–6 | Takes 10 minutes to make, 45 minutes to cook**

**2 tbsp vegetable or olive oil**
**1 onion, finely chopped**
**1 carrot, diced**
**1 stick celery, diced**
**1 clove garlic, chopped**
**150g dried red lentils**
**400g can chopped tomatoes**
**1 litre vegetable stock**
**2 tbsp tomato purée**
**1 bay leaf**
**salt and freshly ground black pepper**
**grated Cheddar cheese, to serve (optional)**

In a large saucepan, heat the oil and gently sweat the onion, carrot, celery and garlic for around 5 minutes or until softened a little.

Stir through the lentils and pour in the tomatoes and stock. Bring up to a steady simmer, add the tomato purée and bay leaf and cook, uncovered, for around 35–45 minutes or until the lentils are soft and collapsing. Do not add any salt when you add the bay leaf, as it will prevent the lentils cooking softly, but do season with plenty of freshly ground black pepper at that stage.

Once the lentils are cooked, you can season to taste with salt, then either purée the soup a little using a stick blender in the pan or leave as a more rustic soup.

Sometimes I serve this soup with a sprinkle of grated Cheddar on top; sometimes I like it simple and unadorned. The choice is yours.

**This soup freezes very well (so is a good soup for batch cooking) – freeze for up to 3 months. Defrost thoroughly, then reheat gently until piping hot. See page 8 for more guidance on this.**

# Mulligatawny

This classic Anglo-Indian dish reminds me of my granddad. He was really keen on the canned Heinz stuff and having spent time in India as a child, I think it must have reminded him of the colonial days. There are countless recipes for mulligatawny, containing lamb, chicken or simply vegetables. Mine contains minced beef, as a nod to granddad and his love of Heinz.

**Serves 4–6 | Takes 15 minutes to make, 15 minutes to cook**

1 tbsp vegetable oil
200g minced beef
1 onion, finely chopped
1 carrot, diced
3 cloves garlic, crushed
2–3 tbsp medium-hot curry paste
2 tbsp plain flour
1.5 litres beef stock (opposite)
100g creamed coconut, roughly chopped
4 tbsp white basmati rice, rinsed
1 tbsp tomato purée
salt and freshly ground black pepper
mango chutney and chapattis or other flatbread, to serve

In a large, heavy-based saucepan, heat the oil and fry the mince over a medium-high heat for 5–10 minutes or until brown and lightly caramelised. Add the onion, carrot and garlic and fry for a further couple of minutes. Stir through the curry paste and flour, mixing well to break up any lumps.

Pour in the stock and bring up to the boil. Reduce the heat to a steady simmer and stir through the creamed coconut, rice and tomato purée. Cook, uncovered, for 10–15 minutes or until the vegetables and rice are tender. Season to taste with salt and freshly ground black pepper.

Serve with a spoonful of mango chutney on top and chapattis on the side to dip in.

**This soup freezes well – freeze for up to 3 months. Defrost thoroughly, then reheat gently until piping hot. See page 8 for more guidance on this.**

**Basic Beef or Lamb Stock**
3kg raw beef, lamb or mutton bones
1.5kg mixed vegetables (such as onions, carrots and celery), chopped
1 whole head garlic, cloves separated but unpeeled
3 bay leaves
generous handful of fresh herbs (such as thyme, a little sage or rosemary and parsley)
1 tsp black peppercorns

Preheat the oven until it is very hot – about 240°C/gas 9. Lay the meat bones in a single layer on 1 or 2 baking sheets and roast in the oven for 50–60 minutes, turning them regularly to ensure even browning. Add the vegetables and roast for a further 20 minutes, stirring them 2 or 3 times to prevent burning. Reduce the oven temperature to 140°C/gas 1. Transfer all the bones and roast vegetables to a stock-pot. Add a little water to the roasting tin and heat over a gentle flame, scraping the bottom to release all the sticky caramelised bits that will add so much flavour. Pour into the pan and add a further 2 litres cold water, together with the garlic, herbs and peppercorns. Bring slowly up to the boil, cover tightly with a lid or with a tight-fitting piece of foil, then transfer the stock-pot to the oven and cook for 6 hours. Alternatively, once the stock ingredients have come to the boil, reduce the heat to a gentle simmer and cook, uncovered, for 6 hours. Strain and allow to cool, then refrigerate overnight, after which the fat will have risen and solidified on the surface. Remove and discard the fat. Use the stock as required or store in a covered container in the fridge and use within 3 days. The stock can be frozen for up to 3 months (see page 8 for more guidance on freezing).

# Winter Lamb and Vegetable Soup

This simple and warming soup contains pearl barley to make it even more substantial and hearty. It's a lovely and nourishing meal in a bowl for a cold winter's day. It really needs no accompaniment, but crusty bread with plenty of butter would be a real treat.

**Serves 4–6 | Takes 15 minutes to make, 1 hour to cook**

**1 tbsp olive oil**
**300g lamb neck fillet, cut into bite-sized pieces**
**2 onions, roughly chopped**
**300g potatoes, cut into chunks**
**2 carrots, cut into chunks**
**$^{1}/_{2}$ swede, cut into chunks**
**75g pearl barley**
**2 tsp dried mixed herbs**
**1.5 litres beef or lamb stock**
**salt and freshly ground black pepper**

Heat the oil in a large, heavy-based saucepan and fry the lamb quickly until golden brown all over. Add the onions, potatoes, carrots and swede and fry for a further couple of minutes.

Stir through the pearl barley and herbs, then pour over the stock. Bring up to the boil and simmer steadily, uncovered, for around 1 hour or until the lamb and barley are tender. By this time, the vegetables should have broken down a little and the soup thickened. If the soup has become too thick, simply add a little more stock or water.

Season to taste with salt and plenty of freshly ground black pepper and serve.

**This soup freezes well, although the vegetables will break down even further on reheating, so you may need to add even more stock or water at this stage. This soup will freeze for up to 3 months. Defrost thoroughly, then reheat gently until piping hot. See page 8 for more guidance on this.**

# Spring Greens Broth with Pork and Lemon Meatballs

I love meatballs in all their incarnations – they are cheap and easy to make, and when seasoned properly, are really very tasty. I do think it's important to cook and taste a little of the mixture to check they are not bland before you go to the trouble of rolling them all out. Warm crusty ciabatta bread is the perfect accompaniment.

**Serves 4–6 | Takes 25 minutes to make, 15 minutes to cook**

**For the meatballs**
**500g minced pork**
**80g fresh breadcrumbs**
**1 small onion, finely chopped**
**finely grated zest of 1 large lemon**
**2 cloves garlic, finely chopped**
**3 tbsp finely chopped fresh mixed herbs (a mix of thyme, rosemary and sage is lovely)**
**1 egg**
**4 tbsp vegetable oil, for frying**
**salt and freshly ground black pepper**

**For the soup**
**2 tbsp olive oil**
**1 large onion, sliced**
**2 cloves garlic, sliced**
**1 litre chicken stock**
**2 heads of spring greens, finely sliced**
**small bunch of fresh flat-leaf parsley, roughly chopped**
**40g fresh Parmesan cheese, finely grated, extra virgin olive oil and warm ciabatta bread, to serve**

For the meatballs, mix the mince with the breadcrumbs, onion, lemon zest, garlic, herbs and egg in a bowl. Season generously with salt and freshly ground black pepper. Take a little pinch of the mixture and roll it into a ball. Fry in a little of the vegetable oil in a large frying pan until crisp and cooked through, then taste to check the seasoning and adjust, if necessary. Once you are happy with the taste, roll the rest of the meatball mixture into walnut-sized balls.

Heat the remaining vegetable oil in the frying pan and fry the meatballs in batches until golden brown and cooked through – this will take about 10 minutes over a medium-high heat – setting each batch aside on a plate when it is done. Set the meatballs aside and keep warm in a low oven whilst you prepare the soup.

For the soup, heat the olive oil in a large saucepan and gently fry the onion for 10 minutes or until it is soft and translucent. Add the garlic and fry for a further minute before pouring over the stock. Bring up to a steady simmer, then add the spring greens and parsley and cook, uncovered, until the greens are just tender – this will take around 5–10 minutes. Season to taste with salt and freshly ground black pepper.

Serve the broth with the meatballs scattered on top, sprinkled with a little Parmesan and a generous drizzle of extra virgin olive oil. Serve with warm ciabatta bread.

**The raw meatballs are suitable for freezing; the soup is not suitable for freezing. Wrap and freeze the raw meatballs for up to 3 months. Defrost thoroughly, then cook as directed. Soup not suitable for freezing, so make this fresh and serve with the cooked meatballs.**

# Chicken Broth with Vermicelli

Loosely based on the traditional Jewish clear chicken soup – otherwise known as Jewish penicillin – this really restorative and comforting dish is great for days when you feel a little out of sorts. The flavour from this soup comes almost entirely from the stock, so it is best to use free-range or organic chicken, if possible, as these more mature birds will yield far more in the taste department. Shred a little of the poached chicken into the soup as a garnish, then allow the rest to cool and save for really succulent sandwiches or salads.

**Serves 4–6 | Takes 10 minutes to make, 1 hour 40 minutes to cook**

**For the stock**
**1.5kg oven-ready chicken, preferably free-range or organic**
**2 carrots, cut into large chunks**
**2 sticks celery, cut in half**
**1 onion, unpeeled, cut into quarters**
**small bunch of fresh flat-leaf parsley**
**1 tsp whole black peppercorns**
**$\frac{1}{2}$ tsp ground mace**

**For the soup**
**150g dried vermicelli**
**1 carrot, thinly sliced into discs**
**100g frozen peas (no need to defrost)**
**salt and freshly ground black pepper**
**a little of the shredded poached chicken, to serve**

Make the stock by placing all the ingredients in a large stock-pot. Cover with cold water and bring slowly to the boil. Simmer as gently as possible, uncovered, for 1½ hours, taking care not to let the stock boil fast or the resulting stock will be cloudy. Skim off any scum that rises to the surface during simmering.

Remove the poached chicken to a large plate and leave to cool – use the cooked chicken for sandwiches, salads, etc.

Meanwhile, sieve the stock into a clean saucepan, discarding the vegetables, herbs and spices.

For the soup, add the vermicelli, carrot and peas to the stock in the pan and simmer, uncovered, for around 8–10 minutes or until the pasta and vegetables are tender. Season to taste with salt and freshly ground black pepper.

Serve the soup with a few strips of shredded poached chicken floating on top of each portion.

**Not suitable for freezing.**

# Oxtail Soup

I have to admit most of my memories of oxtail soup revolve around the canned stuff that seemed to be popular when I was a child. If I think hard I can remember the taste of it now, and not particularly fondly I'm afraid. This, however, is the real deal – a rich meaty broth studded with finely shredded pieces of succulent meat. It does take a long time to prepare, but as most of that time involves gentle simmering on the hob, it's really not too much of an effort.

**Serves 4–6 | Takes 30 minutes to make, 3 hours to cook**

**1kg oxtail, preferably from the thick end, cut into rings**
**3 tbsp plain flour, seasoned with salt and freshly ground black pepper**
**2 tbsp vegetable oil**
**2 onions, finely chopped**
**2 carrots, finely chopped**
**2 sticks celery, finely chopped**
**2 litres good quality beef stock**
**250ml red wine**
**2 tbsp tomato purée**
**2 bay leaves**

In a large bowl, toss the oxtail pieces in the seasoned flour until they are coated all over. Heat the oil in a deep, heavy-based saucepan and sear the oxtail quickly over a high heat until golden brown. Do this in batches, if necessary, to avoid overcrowding the pan, transferring each batch to a plate and continuing until all the pieces are done.

Lower the heat a little, add the onions, carrots and celery and fry for a few minutes until slightly softened. Return the oxtail to the pan, along with any remaining seasoned flour from the plate. Pour over the stock and wine and bring up to a gentle simmer.

Stir through the tomato purée and add the bay leaves, then cover with a lid and cook over a low heat for 2½ –3 hours or until the oxtail is so tender it is falling off the bone – the cooking time will depend on the thickness of the oxtail.

Using a slotted spoon, remove the oxtail to a plate, allow to cool a little and then, using your fingers, shred the meat finely, discarding any bone and large pieces of fat.

Carefully pour the rest of the soup into a blender, purée until smooth, then return to the pan, along with the shredded meat. Bring back up to a simmer and taste to see if you need to add any more salt and black pepper. Serve with crusty bread.

**Not suitable for freezing.**

# Roast Squash Soup with Sage and Brie

I often buy butternut squash seduced, I think, by their lovely curvy shape, only to leave them lurking in the veg basket for weeks. Lucky for me that they keep so well. This soup may be the answer to my dreams, so easy and so autumnal, it makes a perfect quick lunch on the first chilly days at the end of summer.

**Serves 4–6 | Takes 20–25 minutes to make, 10 minutes to cook**

**1 large butternut squash (about 1–1.2kg), peeled, deseeded and cut into 2cm chunks**
**4 tbsp olive oil**
**handful of fresh sage leaves, roughly chopped**
**3 cloves garlic, unpeeled**
**1 litre vegetable or chicken stock**
**salt and freshly ground black pepper**
**120–180g firm brie, cut into cubes, to serve**
**a little chopped fresh sage, to garnish**

Preheat the oven to 200°C/gas 6.

In a large roasting tin, toss the squash in the oil and sage, then add the garlic cloves. Season with a little salt and freshly ground black pepper and roast in the oven for 20–25 minutes or until the squash is tender and starting to caramelise at the edges.

Carefully tip half of the roast squash into a blender, along with all of the stock. Squeeze the garlic cloves out of their skins (discarding the skins), then add them to the blender and purée until smooth.

Pour into a pan along with the remaining roast squash pieces and bring up to a simmer. Taste to check the seasoning, adding a little more salt and black pepper, if necessary.

Serve the soup with the brie scattered over and a little extra sage sprinkled on top to garnish.

**This soup does freeze (without the brie garnish) but the lumps of squash tend to be a bit soggy on defrosting, so if you plan to freeze it you may want to purée the whole soup to smooth. Do not freeze with the brie garnish. The soup will freeze for up to 3 months. Defrost thoroughly, then reheat gently until piping hot. See page 8 for more guidance on this.**

# Italian Bean and Pasta Soup

Based on the traditional Italian soup, Pasta e Fagioli, this is a simple, filling and cheap dish to make. I like to add a generous handful of torn basil leaves at the end of cooking, which although not particularly authentic, wakes up the flavour no end. It's worth using good fresh Parmesan and extra virgin olive oil at the end to elevate the dish from frugal to delicious.

**Serves 4–6 | Takes 15 minutes to make, plus overnight soaking of the beans, 1 hour 20 minutes to cook**

**150g dried cannellini beans, soaked overnight in cold water, drained and rinsed**
**1 onion, finely chopped**
**2 tbsp olive oil**
**2 cloves garlic, crushed**
**1 carrot, finely diced**
**2 tbsp tomato purée**
**2 x 400g cans chopped tomatoes**
**2 litres vegetable stock**
**2 bay leaves**
**150g dried short pasta, such as macaroni**
**large bunch of fresh basil leaves, roughly torn**
**salt and freshly ground black pepper**
**40g fresh Parmesan cheese, finely grated, and extra virgin olive oil, to serve**

In a large saucepan, gently fry the onion in the olive oil for about 5 minutes or until softened. Add the garlic and carrot and fry for another couple of minutes.

Stir through the drained cannellini beans and tomato purée, then pour in the tomatoes and stock. Add the bay leaves and season with plenty of freshly ground black pepper. Do not add any salt at this stage, as it will toughen up the bean skins.

Bring up to the boil and boil rapidly for 10 minutes. Lower the heat to a steady simmer and continue to cook, uncovered, until the beans are soft and tender – this will take around 1 hour. Add a little more water or stock if it is getting too dry.

Stir in the pasta and simmer, uncovered, for a further 10 minutes or so until it is cooked through but still with a little bite.

Remove from the heat, stir through the basil and season to taste with salt and perhaps a little more black pepper.

Serve the soup in bowls, sprinkled with the Parmesan and a generous drizzle of extra virgin olive oil.

**This soup freezes very well without the basil (the basil will blacken when frozen), so simply add the basil after reheating. This soup will freeze for up to 3 months. Defrost thoroughly, then reheat gently until piping hot. See page 8 for more guidance on this.**

# Cream of Leek Soup with Cider and Cheddar

**This Somerset-inspired creamy soup is ideal to make in the winter when leeks are at their best and are cheap. Served with warm crusty bread, this is a delicious warming lunch to offer to friends.**

**Serves 4–6 | Takes 15 minutes to make, 20 minutes to cook**

**50g unsalted butter**
**850g leeks (about 3 fat ones or 5 smaller ones), washed and sliced**
**2 sprigs of fresh thyme or 1 tsp dried thyme**
**750ml chicken or vegetable stock**
**250ml dry cider**
**2 tbsp plain flour**
**1 tbsp English mustard (either powder or ready-mixed paste)**
**150ml single cream**
**150g mature Cheddar cheese, grated**
**salt and freshly ground black pepper**

Melt the butter gently in a large, heavy-based saucepan and sweat the leeks with the thyme for 10–15 minutes or until they have softened. Be careful not to let the leeks burn, otherwise they will taste bitter, so keep a close eye on them, adding a tablespoon of water if they look like they might catch.

When the leeks are soft, pour in the stock and cider and season with a little salt and freshly ground black pepper. Bring up to the boil, then lower the heat and simmer, uncovered, until the leeks are completely cooked through. I find this takes a little longer than you might think – a good 15 minutes or so.

Carefully pour half of the soup into a blender, add the flour and mustard and purée until smooth, then return to the pan and stir well to mix together. Bring up to a simmer and cook for a few minutes to thicken the soup, stirring.

Reduce the heat to a minimum, pour in the cream and add the cheese, stirring well until the cheese has melted. Reheat gently until hot but do not boil otherwise the soup may separate slightly.

Taste to check the seasoning, adding a little more salt and black pepper, if necessary. Serve with crusty bread.

**Not suitable for freezing.**

# Sweet Potato Soup with Crisp Chilli Beef

**I was really thrilled when I first made this soup, which to my mind is a triumph of contrasting textures and flavours. Sweet potatoes make a soup with a beautiful, velvety smooth texture and a mild flavour, which gets transformed by a punchy topping of crisp spicy beef. I adore chilli so I use a fiery habanero chilli sauce, which is really quite addictive.**

**Serves 4–6 | Takes 15 minutes to make, 15 minutes to cook**

**2 tbsp olive oil**
**2 onions, finely chopped**
**2 cloves garlic, crushed**
**800g sweet potatoes, cut into 2cm chunks**
**1 litre vegetable or chicken stock**
**salt and freshly ground black pepper**

**For the crisp chilli beef**
**2 tbsp olive oil**
**225g lean minced beef**
**2 tsp cumin seeds, coarsely ground**
**1 tsp Spanish smoked paprika**
**2 cloves garlic, crushed**
**hot chilli sauce (such as Tabasco), to taste**

Heat the oil in a large saucepan and fry the onions for around 10 minutes until soft and lightly caramelised. Add the garlic and sweet potatoes and fry for a further minute, before pouring in the stock.

Bring up to the boil, then lower the heat and simmer, uncovered, until the potatoes are really soft and almost collapsing – this will take about 15 minutes, depending on the size of your potato chunks.

Whilst the soup is simmering, make the crisp chilli beef. Place a large frying pan over a high heat and pour in the oil. When it is smoking hot, fry the mince, breaking up the meat into little strands with a wooden spoon. It's important to keep the heat as high as possible and to keep the meat moving, just as if you were making a stir-fry. When the mince is crisp and golden, add the cumin, smoked paprika, garlic and chilli sauce to taste, and fry for a further minute. Turn the heat off and leave to rest whilst you finish the soup.

Carefully pour the soup into a blender and purée until completely smooth. Return to the pan and season to taste with a little salt and freshly ground black pepper, then reheat gently until hot.

Serve the hot soup with the crisp chilli beef sprinkled over the top.

**This soup freezes well (without the chilli beef garnish) – freeze for up to 3 months. Defrost thoroughly, then reheat gently until piping hot. See page 8 for more guidance on this. Crisp chilli beef not suitable for freezing, so make this as the soup is reheating.**

# EXHILARATING

There are soups that soothe and calm and there are soups that do the polar opposite – they invigorate, vitalize and wake-up the senses. A hint of chilli, generous handfuls of roughly chopped summer herbs, a big squeeze of citrus juice or the zing of freshly grated ginger – these are soups we turn to when we want to be lifted and energized. The soups in this chapter take their inspiration from around the globe, many fragrant with spices, others heady with fresh herbs.

# Gingered Pork and Pak Choi Soup

Plenty of fresh ginger really makes this soup sing loud and clear, creating the perfect pick-me-up for those slightly jaded days we all have from time to time. The addition of the noodles and pork make this substantial enough for a healthy, light main course. With this broth-style soup, it is worth using homemade chicken stock if you have some in the freezer, otherwise use good quality ready-made stock.

**Serves 4–6 | Takes 10 minutes to make, plus 2–3 hours (or overnight) marinating, 15–20 minutes to cook**

**For the marinade and pork**
**4–5cm piece of fresh root ginger, peeled and grated**
**2 cloves garlic, crushed**
**2 tbsp kecap manis (Indonesian sweet soy sauce), or if unavailable, use dark soy sauce instead**
**1 tbsp honey**
**1 tbsp tomato ketchup**
**1 tbsp sweet chilli sauce**
**1 pork tenderloin (fillet), weighing 400–500g**

**For the soup**
**800ml homemade chicken stock or good quality ready-made chicken stock**
**1 lemongrass stalk, cut in half lengthways and bruised with the back of a knife**
**2 fresh red chillies, deseeded and finely sliced**
**2 heads of pak choi, roughly chopped**
**2 blocks of dried egg noodles (about 150g in total)**
**loose handful of fresh coriander leaves, roughly chopped**

In a large, non-metallic bowl, mix all the marinade ingredients (except the pork) together. Cut a few slashes on both sides of the pork tenderloin to help the marinade penetrate the meat, then add the pork to the marinade and rub the marinade into the meat well. Place on a plate, cover with cling film and chill in the fridge for a good 2–3 hours, or overnight if possible.

When you are ready to make the soup, remove the pork from the marinade, scraping off as much marinade as you can, and reserve it. Heat a griddle or frying pan until really hot and fry the pork on all sides for around 12–15 minutes or until crisp and cooked through, turning occasionally. Reduce the heat a little if it is starting to colour too much. Remove to a plate and keep hot. Just before serving, thickly slice the pork across the grain.

Whilst the pork is cooking, pour the stock into a large saucepan and add the reserved marinade, along with the lemongrass and chillies. Bring up to the boil, then lower the heat and simmer, uncovered, for 10 minutes. Add the pak choi, noodles and coriander and stir until the noodles separate, then simmer for a further 5 minutes or until the noodles are cooked.

Remove and discard the lemongrass. Pour the soup into deep bowls and top with slices of the cooked pork. Serve immediately.

**Soup is not suitable for freezing. You can freeze the marinated uncooked pork, if you like – freeze for up to 3 months. Defrost thoroughly before cooking as directed. See page 8 for more guidance on freezing.**

# Chicken Squash Soup

This Indonesian-inspired soup is topped with lovely crunchy satay sauce to stir through as you eat. A few years ago, I was lucky enough to spend a lot of time working in Indonesia and I completely fell in love with the hot, sweet and sour cuisine, which I often try to recreate at home, bringing back memories of humid nights and fragrant suppers.

**Serves 4–6 | Takes 25 minutes to make, 15 minutes to cook**

**For the satay sauce**
**150g salted peanuts**
**1 tbsp vegetable oil**
**2 shallots, finely chopped**
**4 cloves garlic, finely chopped**
**2–3 fresh red birdseye chillies, deseeded and finely chopped**
**$^1/_2$ tsp shrimp paste**
**165ml coconut milk**
**1 tbsp jaggery (raw cane sugar) or light soft brown sugar**
**2 tsp kecap manis (Indonesian sweet soy sauce), or if unavailable, use dark soy sauce instead, plus 1 extra tsp jaggery**
**juice of $^1/_2$–1 lime, or to taste**

**For the soup**
**2 tbsp vegetable oil**
**6 shallots, finely chopped**
**3 cloves garlic, crushed**
**4 skinless, boneless chicken thighs, cut into bite-sized pieces**
**1 litre chicken stock**
**400g butternut squash, peeled, deseeded and cut into 2cm cubes**
**4 frozen or dried kaffir lime leaves, finely sliced**
**2–3 fresh red birdseye chillies, deseeded and finely sliced**
**2 lemongrass stalks, finely chopped**
**salt and freshly ground black pepper**
**small bunch of fresh coriander, leaves roughly chopped, to garnish**

Begin by making the satay sauce. Using a pestle and mortar or a mini food processor, grind the peanuts to form coarse crumbs. Set aside. Heat the oil in a small saucepan and fry the shallots and garlic with the chillies over a low heat for about 10 minutes or until soft and golden.

Stir in the shrimp paste, coconut milk, jaggery and kecap manis. Add the ground peanuts, bring up to a gentle simmer, then cook, uncovered, for 3–4 minutes or until thickened. Remove from the heat and add the lime juice to taste – it should be hot, sweet, salty and sour. Set aside to cool to room temperature.

To make the soup, heat the oil in a heavy-based saucepan and gently fry the shallots and garlic for about 5 minutes or until lightly caramelised. Add the chicken and stir-fry for a few minutes until sealed all over.

Pour in the stock, add the butternut squash and stir through the lime leaves, chillies and lemongrass. Bring up to the boil, then reduce the heat to a steady simmer and cook, uncovered, for around 10 minutes or until the chicken is cooked and the squash is tender.

Season to taste with salt and freshly ground black pepper. Serve the soup in bowls with a generous dollop of satay sauce on top of each portion and a sprinkling of chopped coriander.

**This soup and the satay sauce are both suitable for freezing. Freeze them separately – freeze for up to 3 months. Defrost the soup and satay sauce thoroughly, then reheat the soup gently until piping hot. See page 8 for more guidance on this. Reheat the satay sauce, adding a little extra water, until hot, then cool to room temperature before serving with the soup (see recipe).**

# Thai Prawn, Lime and Coconut Soup

**This soup is packed full of all the classic Thai flavours – lemongrass, lime and creamy coconut milk – and it is really quick and easy to make. I like my food spicy, so I usually add plenty of red curry paste to the soup and a generous scattering of sliced fresh chillies as a garnish.**

**Serves 4–6 | Takes 10 minutes to make, 15 minutes to cook**

**1 tbsp vegetable oil**
**6 shallots, finely sliced**
**2 cloves garlic, crushed**
**2 lemongrass stalks, cut in half lengthways and bruised with the back of a knife**
**1 red pepper, deseeded and thinly sliced**
**250g green beans, cut in half**
**750ml chicken stock**
**400ml can coconut milk**
**2–3 tbsp Thai red curry paste, or to taste**
**2 tbsp fish sauce (nam pla)**
**2 tsp jaggery (raw cane sugar) or light soft brown sugar**
**4 tbsp white basmati rice or Thai jasmine rice, rinsed**
**400g raw peeled king prawns, cut in half lengthways**
**juice of 1 lime**
**salt and freshly ground black pepper**
**4 spring onions, finely sliced, 2 fresh red birdseye chillies, deseeded and finely sliced, and small bunch of fresh coriander, roughly chopped, to serve**

Heat the oil in a large saucepan and gently sweat the shallots for 5 minutes or until they soften. Add the garlic and lemongrass and cook for a further minute, before stirring through the red pepper and green beans. Pour in the chicken stock and coconut milk and bring up to the boil.

Turn the heat down to a steady simmer and stir through the red curry paste, fish sauce and jaggery. Add the rice, then simmer, uncovered, for 10–12 minutes, by which time the rice should be almost cooked and the vegetables tender.

Finally, stir through the prawns and cook for a further few minutes or until they are pink and cooked all the way through. Squeeze in the juice of the lime and taste to check the seasoning – you may need to add a little salt and freshly ground black pepper. Remove and discard the lemongrass.

Serve the soup immediately in bowls, scattered with the spring onions, chillies and chopped coriander.

**Not suitable for freezing.**

# Hot Sweetcorn Soup (Sopa de Maize)

This recipe comes from my great mate, Jo Ingleby, who's a real wizard in the kitchen. One of the many things we have in common is a love of spicy food from the far corners of the world, and this soup is no exception, hailing from Mexico where it is known simply as sopa de maize – maize soup. If you prefer things a touch less fiery, reduce the quantity of red chilli, or simply leave out the green chilli garnish.

**Serves 4–6 | Takes 15 minutes to make, 20 minutes to cook**

1 tbsp cumin seeds
1 tsp coriander seeds
2 tbsp sunflower oil
2 large onions, finely chopped
1 stick celery, finely chopped
1 red pepper, deseeded and chopped
1–2 hot fresh red chillies, deseeded and chopped
2 cloves garlic, crushed
2 bay leaves
1 tsp paprika (unsmoked)
1 litre vegetable stock
500g frozen sweetcorn kernels (no need to defrost)
1 fresh corn on the cob
3 tbsp roughly chopped fresh coriander
juice of 1 lime
salt and freshly ground black pepper
3 tbsp sour cream, 1 fresh green chilli, finely chopped, and a little chopped fresh coriander, to garnish
lime wedges and warmed soft flour tortillas, to serve

In a small frying pan, dry-fry the cumin and coriander seeds for a minute or two. As soon as you smell their aroma wafting up from the pan, tip them into a pestle and mortar and grind together. Set aside.

Heat the oil in a large saucepan and fry the onions and celery for 10 minutes or so until the vegetables have softened and are just starting to caramelise. Add the red pepper, red chillies, garlic, bay leaves and paprika, along with the ground cumin and coriander. Fry for a further couple of minutes.

Pour in the stock and stir through the frozen sweetcorn. Bring up to the boil, then lower the heat and simmer gently, uncovered, for 20 minutes.

Whilst the soup is cooking, preheat the grill until it is really hot, then grill the corn on the cob until it is slightly blackened all over. You could use a BBQ to do this for a lovely smoky taste, if you like – in fact, this is a great soup for any BBQ leftovers. Remove from the heat and use a sharp knife to carefully slice the kernels off the cob.

Remove the bay leaves from the soup and discard, then stir in the chopped coriander. Purée the soup to the desired consistency using a stick blender in the pan. Add the grilled sweetcorn kernels and lime juice, then season to taste with salt and freshly ground black pepper.

Serve immediately in bowls, garnishing each portion with a swirl of sour cream and a scattering of green chilli and chopped coriander. Pass around wedges of lime for people to squeeze in as they eat and serve with warmed tortillas.

**This soup freezes well (without the garnishes) – freeze for up to 3 months. Defrost thoroughly, then reheat gently until piping hot. See page 8 for more guidance on this. Garnishes not suitable for freezing, so simply add these just before serving.**

# Vietnamese Pho (Spiced Beef, Noodle and Vegetable Soup)

**In Vietnam, this classic clear broth is eaten for breakfast. Very thin slices of raw beef are lightly cooked when the hot broth is poured over them – chill the beef in the freezer for 30 minutes or so beforehand to make slicing easier. Although it looks like a lot of effort, most of the time spent to make this soup is preparing the spiced broth, which can be left alone in a low oven for the day. The soup is then ready in a matter of minutes.**

**Serves 4–6 | Takes 15 minutes to make, plus 8 hours cooking the broth, 10 minutes to cook the soup**

**For the beef broth**
**2kg beef bones (a mix of knuckle, leg, marrow, oxtail – ask your butcher)**
**2 onions, unpeeled, cut into quarters**
**5cm piece of fresh root ginger, unpeeled and roughly chopped**
**1 tbsp coriander seeds**
**1 tbsp fennel seeds**
**1 tbsp whole cardamom pods**
**1 tbsp black peppercorns**
**6 cloves**
**4 star anise**
**3 tbsp fish sauce (nam pla), plus extra for seasoning**

**For the soup**
**250g dried wide flat rice noodles**
**8 spring onions, sliced on the diagonal**
**300g fillet, sirloin or rib-eye steak, very thinly sliced**

**For the garnishes**
**small bunch each of fresh coriander and fresh mint, leaves roughly chopped**
**2 limes, cut into wedges**
**4 fresh red birdseye chillies, deseeded and finely sliced**

Start the broth 8 hours before you want to eat the soup. Preheat the oven to 110°C/gas ¼ .

Put the beef bones into a large, ovenproof stock-pot and cover with cold water. Bring up to the boil and simmer, uncovered, for 10 minutes, skimming off any scum with a slotted spoon. Remove from the heat and drain, discarding the water, then rinse the bones in cold running water. This will ultimately give you a clearer broth.

Rinse out the stock-pot, return the bones to the pot and re-cover with 2 litres of fresh cold water. Add the onions, fresh ginger, spices and fish sauce and bring up to a gentle simmer. Cover with a tight-fitting lid or a double layer of foil, transfer to the oven and cook, undisturbed, for 8 hours.

When you are ready to make the soup, strain the broth into a clean saucepan and discard all the bones, spices, etc. Add the noodles to the broth, stirring until they separate, then simmer for a few minutes until cooked. Stir through the spring onions and taste – you may want to add a splash more fish sauce.

Serve the soup by dividing the thinly sliced beef between deep bowls. Pour the hot broth and noodles over the top and serve immediately. Serve the garnishes – chopped herbs, lime wedges and chillies – in small bowls alongside for each person to garnish their own soup.

**Not suitable for freezing.**

# Balinese Yellow Seafood Soup

The key to this dish is the yellow curry paste, which you can buy ready-made in oriental supermarkets. However, I would urge you to make it fresh as it tastes wonderful and is so different from the ubiquitous red curry paste we are more familiar with. The list of ingredients is long but it's really very easy to make. You will end up with twice as much as you need for the soup, but it will keep (in a covered container) for a week or so in the fridge or for up to 1 month in the freezer, and it makes a great marinade for chicken or fish.

**Serves 4–6 | Takes 15 minutes to make, 15 minutes to cook**

**For the Balinese yellow curry paste**
1 tbsp coriander seeds
1 tsp sesame seeds
1 tsp black peppercorns
1 tsp cumin seeds
4 cloves
$\frac{1}{2}$ tsp freshly grated nutmeg
10 shallots, roughly chopped
4 cloves garlic, roughly chopped
2 lemongrass stalks, chopped
2 medium-hot fresh red chillies, deseeded and chopped
2 fresh red birdseye chillies, deseeded and chopped
5cm piece of galangal, peeled and roughly chopped (if unavailable, substitute fresh root ginger)
5cm piece of fresh root ginger, peeled and roughly chopped
10cm piece of fresh turmeric root, peeled and chopped (if unavailable, substitute 2 generous tbsp dried ground turmeric)
40g salted peanuts
4 tbsp vegetable oil
1 tbsp jaggery (raw cane sugar) or light soft brown sugar
1 tsp dried shrimp paste

**For the soup**
2 tbsp vegetable oil
8 generous tbsp Balinese yellow curry paste (see above)
4 frozen or dried kaffir lime leaves, finely chopped
600ml fish or vegetable stock
400ml can coconut milk
250g skinless white fish fillets (such as cod or haddock), cut into bite-sized pieces
200g raw peeled king prawns, cut in half lengthways
juice of 1–2 limes, or to taste
salt and freshly ground black pepper

First, make the yellow curry paste. Grind the coriander seeds, sesame seeds, peppercorns, cumin seeds, cloves and nutmeg together in a spice mill. Put all the other paste ingredients into a food processor, along with the ground spices, and whizz together until you have a smooth paste. Set aside.

For the soup, heat the oil in a large saucepan and gently fry the spice paste until it starts to smell fragrant. Add the lime leaves, stock and coconut milk and bring gently to the boil, then simmer gently, uncovered, for 10 minutes.

Stir through the fish and prawns and simmer until they are cooked through – this will take about another 5 minutes. Squeeze in the lime juice to taste and season with a little salt and freshly ground black pepper. Serve immediately.

**This soup is best made fresh, so is not suitable for freezing. Yellow curry paste freezes well for up to 1 month. Defrost thoroughly before use. See page 8 for more guidance on freezing.**

# Red Pepper with Peri Peri Prawns

Peri peri (or piri piri) is a sauce familiar to many of us these days, thanks to a chain of Portuguese chilli-chicken fast food restaurants. Peri peri translates as 'pepper pepper' in Swahili and it actually refers to a small type of chilli pepper. Columbus brought these chillies home after his travels to the new world, and from Portugal they made their way to Africa on the trade routes where they were presumably named.

Serves 4–6 | Takes 10 minutes to make, plus 30 minutes marinating, 12–15 minutes to cook

**For the peri peri prawns**
**200g raw peeled king prawns**
**1 long fresh red chilli, deseeded and finely chopped**
**1 tsp paprika (unsmoked)**
**2 cloves garlic, crushed**
**2cm piece of fresh root ginger, peeled and finely grated**
**2 tbsp olive oil, plus extra for frying**
**juice of 1 lemon**

**For the soup**
**2 tbsp olive oil**
**3 large red peppers, deseeded and chopped**
**2 onions, chopped**
**3 cloves garlic, crushed**
**800ml vegetable stock**
**2 heaped tbsp natural Greek-style yogurt**
**salt and freshly ground black pepper**
**handful of fresh coriander leaves, roughly chopped, to garnish**

Firstly, marinate the prawns. 'Butterfly' the prawns by scoring each one lightly down the back with a sharp knife – this will allow more of the marinade to soak in and they look pretty as they open up when you cook them. In a non-metallic bowl, mix the prawns with the chilli, paprika, garlic, ginger and oil. Cover and set aside in the fridge for 30 minutes.

Begin the soup by heating the oil in a heavy-based saucepan until it is really hot, then add the peppers and onions and fry over a high heat for around 5 minutes. Stir from time to time, but not too often – you are trying to caramelise, even slightly char, the edges of the vegetables to enhance the flavour.

Add the garlic, stir once, then almost immediately carefully pour over the stock. The pan will be really hot, so it's important to get the stock in quickly before the garlic burns. Take care, the stock may hiss and spit as it comes into contact with the pan. Bring up to the boil, then lower the heat and simmer, uncovered, for 5–8 minutes or until the vegetables are tender.

Carefully transfer the soup to a blender and purée until smooth, then return to the pan. Reheat gently, then remove from the heat, stir through the yogurt and season to taste with salt and freshly ground black pepper. Keep the soup warm but don't let it boil, otherwise the yogurt will separate.

Cook the prawns by heating a little extra oil in a frying pan. When the oil is really hot, add the prawns and stir-fry until cooked through – this will only take a few minutes and they will be pink all the way through when cooked. Remove from the heat and squeeze over the lemon juice.

Serve the soup in bowls with the prawns scattered on top. Garnish each portion with a sprinkling of chopped coriander.

**Not suitable for freezing.**

# Green Chilli Fish Soup

This is a super light and healthy noodle broth where the fish fillets are gently poached on top. The green chilli paste is fresh and fiery – use as much or as little chilli as you like. Although the ingredients list is long, it's a breeze to make as you just whizz it all up in a food processor. As a bonus, the chilli paste also freezes really well, so make double and freeze half to make a green curry at a later date. The chilli paste will also keep in a covered jar (cover surface of paste with a little vegetable oil) in the fridge for up to 3 days.

**Serves 4–6 | Takes 10 minutes to make, plus 30 minutes marinating, 12–15 minutes to cook**

**For the green chilli paste**
**4–6 medium-hot fresh green chillies, deseeded and roughly chopped**
**4 shallots, roughly chopped**
**5cm piece of fresh root ginger, peeled and chopped**
**3 cloves garlic, chopped**
**2 lemongrass stalks, roughly chopped**
**finely grated zest and juice of 1 lime**
**bunch of fresh coriander, leaves and stalks roughly chopped**
**8 frozen or dried kaffir lime leaves (or use the finely grated zest of 1 extra lime)**
**1 tbsp coriander seeds, crushed**
**1 tsp cumin seeds, crushed**
**1 tsp black peppercorns, crushed**

**For the soup**
**4–6 skinless white fish fillets, such as haddock, cod or plaice (about 140g each – allow 1 fillet per portion)**
**2 tbsp vegetable oil**
**1 litre fish or vegetable stock**
**3 blocks of dried egg noodles (about 225g in total)**
**a bunch of spring onions, sliced into 1cm pieces**
**salt and freshly ground black pepper**
**a few fresh coriander leaves, to garnish**

Begin by making the green chilli paste. Put all the paste ingredients into a food processor and whizz together until you have a smooth paste.

For the soup, spread half of the green chilli paste over the fish fillets, then set them aside to marinate at room temperature for 30 minutes.

Once the fish has been marinated, heat the oil in a large, heavy-based saucepan – one large enough to take the fish fillets in a single layer – and add the rest of the chilli paste. Fry gently for a couple of minutes, then pour in the stock. Bring up to the boil, then lower the heat and simmer, uncovered, for 5 minutes. Season to taste with a little salt and perhaps some freshly ground black pepper.

Add the noodles and stir until they separate, then stir through the spring onions. Finally, lay the fish fillets over the top and cover with a lid or tight-fitting piece of foil. Steam the fish on top of the soup until it is just cooked through – this will take around 4–8 minutes, depending on the thickness of the fillets.

To serve, carefully transfer the fish fillets to a plate. Pour the soup into bowls, then lay the fish on top of the soup – serve 1 fish fillet per portion. Garnish with coriander leaves.

**Soup not suitable for freezing but green chilli paste can be frozen for up to 1 month. Defrost thoroughly before use. See page 8 for more guidance on freezing.**

# Singapore Laksa with Salmon

This Malaysian spicy coconut-based noodle soup is wonderfully creamy and fragrant. Although laksa curry paste is readily available from oriental food shops and some supermarkets, I have given a recipe to make your own – it's so simple as everything just gets whizzed together in a food processor, and the homemade stuff will make your soup taste that much fresher. Any leftover laksa paste will keep in a covered container in the fridge for up to 3 days; it will also freeze well for up to 3 months.

**Serves 4–6 | Takes 15 minutes to make, plus 15 minutes soaking the dried shrimps, 15 minutes to cook**

**For the Singapore laksa spice paste**
**5g dried shrimps**
**3 shallots, chopped**
**1 heaped tsp shrimp paste**
**1 tbsp coriander seeds, roughly ground**
**1 lemongrass stalk, finely chopped**
**30g fresh root ginger, peeled and roughly chopped**
**30g fresh turmeric root, peeled and roughly chopped or 2 tsp dried ground turmeric**
**25g salted peanuts**
**2–3 tsp dried chilli flakes**
**3 tbsp vegetable oil**

**For the soup**
**1 tbsp vegetable oil**
**4 tbsp homemade laksa spice paste (see above) or ready-made laksa paste**
**750ml light chicken stock**
**400ml can coconut milk**
**500g skinless salmon fillets, cut into bite-sized chunks**
**250g ready-cooked rice noodles**
**salt, to taste**

**For the garnishes**
**5 spring onions, finely sliced**
**150g piece of cucumber, sliced into thin matchsticks**
**2 fresh red birdseye chillies, deseeded and finely sliced**
**handful of fresh mint leaves, chopped**
**handful of fresh coriander leaves, chopped**
**lime wedges**

To make the laksa spice paste, first put the dried shrimps in a bowl, cover with cold water and leave to soak for 15 minutes, then drain. Place the soaked shrimps and all the remaining paste ingredients in a mini food processor and whizz together to form a fine paste. Set aside.

For the soup, heat the oil in a large saucepan and gently fry the laksa spice paste for a couple of minutes or so until you smell the fragrance wafting up from the pan. Add the stock and coconut milk and bring up to the boil, then lower the heat and simmer, uncovered, for 10 minutes.

Add the salmon and simmer gently for 4–5 minutes or until it is just cooked. Carefully stir through the cooked noodles and allow them to warm through. Add a little salt to taste.

Serve the soup in deep bowls, with the garnishes served alongside in little bowls for people to help themselves.

**Soup not suitable for freezing. Laksa spice paste can be frozen – freeze for up to 3 months. Defrost thoroughly before use. See page 8 for more guidance on freezing.**

# Harissa and Lamb Harira

**Harira is the Moroccan stew-like soup traditionally served to break fasting during Ramadan. I make it with lamb shanks and cook it long and slow in the oven. It's the sort of dish you can get ready in the morning and leave all day, and after such languorous cooking, the lamb simply flakes off the bone. I like to make my own harissa to serve alongside (see recipe on page 107), as the flavour is unbeatable, but if you are short of time, good quality ready-made harissa is a good alternative.**

**Serves 4–6 | Takes 15 minutes to make, plus overnight soaking of the chickpeas, 6 hours to cook**

**100g dried chickpeas, soaked overnight in cold water, drained and rinsed**
**2 tbsp olive oil**
**2 large lamb shanks**
**1 large onion, chopped**
**2–3 cloves garlic, crushed**
**1 tsp ground turmeric**
**1 tsp ground cinnamon**
**$\frac{1}{2}$ tsp ground ginger**
**$\frac{1}{4}$ whole nutmeg, freshly grated**
**4 cloves**
**2 carrots, sliced**
**250g cherry tomatoes, cut in half**
**50g dried green lentils**
**2 litres lamb or vegetable stock**
**2–4 tbsp harissa, or to taste, either ready-made or see page 107 to make your own**
**generous handful of fresh coriander leaves, roughly chopped**
**salt and freshly ground black pepper**
**1 lemon, cut into wedges, to serve**

Preheat the oven to 140°C/gas 1.

Heat the oil in a large, ovenproof saucepan or casserole and fry the lamb shanks all over until golden brown, then remove to a plate and set aside. Reduce the heat a little, then add the onion to the pan and fry for around 10 minutes or until softened and starting to caramelise. Add the garlic, stir through all the spices and fry for a further minute.

Add the carrots, cherry tomatoes, lentils and drained chickpeas. Finally, pour over the stock and bring up to a steady boil, then return the lamb shanks to the pan. Cover tightly with a lid or a snug-fitting piece of foil, then transfer the pan to the oven. Leave to cook for 6 hours or so until the lamb is falling off the bones and the lentils and chickpeas are tender.

Shred the meat off the bones and back into the soup. Discard the bones. Stir the harissa and chopped coriander through the soup and season to taste with salt and freshly ground black pepper.

Serve the soup in deep bowls with the lemon wedges to squeeze over as you eat.

**This soup and the harissa are both suitable for freezing. Freeze them separately – freeze for up to 3 months. Defrost the soup and harissa thoroughly, then reheat the soup gently until piping hot. See page 8 for more guidance on this. Stir the harissa and chopped coriander through the reheated soup just before serving.**

# Shiitake Mushroom and Sichuan Peppercorn Soup

Sichuan pepper adds a pleasing citrusy heat to this super-quick and filling noodle soup. If you want something a little lighter, simply leave the noodles out – it will be just as delicious. I like to use chicken stock for this soup as I think it suits the meaty texture of the mushrooms, but feel free to use vegetable stock, if you prefer.

**Serves 4–6 | Takes 5 minutes to make, 10 minutes to cook**

2 tbsp sesame oil
250g fresh shiitake mushrooms, sliced
2.5cm piece of fresh root ginger, peeled and finely chopped
a bunch of spring onions, sliced
2 cloves garlic, finely sliced
1 medium-hot fresh red chilli, deseeded and finely sliced
1 litre chicken or vegetable stock
2 tbsp dark soy sauce
2 blocks of dried egg noodles (about 150g in total) (optional)
1–2 tsp Sichuan peppercorns, ground using a pestle and mortar
salt, to taste

Heat the oil in a wok and stir-fry the mushrooms with the ginger, spring onions, garlic and chilli for a few minutes or until softened.

Pour in the stock and add the soy sauce, then add the noodles, if you are using them, and stir until they separate. Bring up to the boil, then lower the heat and simmer, uncovered, for 5 minutes.

Stir through the ground Sichuan pepper and season to taste with a little salt. Serve immediately.

**Not suitable for freezing.**

# Mussel, Spinach and Ginger Soup

**Mussels are healthy, cheap and sustainable and I would love it if they were more popular. In this soup, they are added to a broth which is heady with ginger and packed full of nutrient-rich tomatoes and spinach, to create a healthy and delicious bowlful that'll leave you with a real spring in your step.**

**Serves 4–6 | Takes 20 minutes to make, 10 minutes to cook**

**1kg fresh mussels (in shell)**
**1 large onion, finely chopped**
**2 tbsp vegetable oil**
**2 cloves garlic, crushed**
**5cm piece of fresh root ginger, peeled and very finely sliced into matchsticks**
**300g cherry tomatoes, cut in half**
**600ml fish stock (opposite)**
**1 tbsp fish sauce (nam pla)**
**500g fresh spinach, thoroughly washed, drained and roughly chopped**
**salt and freshly ground black pepper**

Prepare the mussels by washing them thoroughly under cold running water. Pull off any beards and discard any mussels that do not shut firmly when tapped against the edge of the sink.

Tip the mussels into a large saucepan and add 300ml cold water. Cover with a tight-fitting lid or piece of foil and bring up to the boil. Cook over a moderate heat, shaking the pan once or twice, for around 5 minutes, by which time the mussels should be cooked and the shells open. Drain and set aside to cool a little, reserving the mussels and cooking juices separately – the cooking juices will add much flavour to the soup. Discard any unopened mussels.

In another large saucepan, gently fry the onion in the oil for 10 minutes – the onion should be soft and translucent but not coloured at all. Add the garlic and ginger and fry for a further minute. Stir through the cherry tomatoes and add the stock and fish sauce.

Pour in the mussel cooking liquor, straining it through a sieve to remove any grit. Bring up to the boil, then lower the heat and simmer, uncovered, for 5 minutes. Add the spinach, cover and simmer for a further 4–5 minutes or until it has wilted. Season to taste with salt and freshly ground black pepper.

Whilst the soup is simmering, remove the mussels from their shells, leaving a few in the shells to garnish. Add the mussels to the soup and warm them through for a minute or two.

Serve the soup in bowls and garnish each portion with 2 or 3 mussels in their shells.

**Not suitable for freezing.**

**Basic Fish Stock**
**1kg raw white fish bones and heads**
**3 sticks celery, chopped**
**2 onions, chopped**
**2 carrots, sliced**
**2 bay leaves, plus a handful of a few other fresh herbs (fennel leaves, and a little dill or parsley are good)**
**1 tsp black peppercorns**
**1 tsp fennel seeds**

Add all the ingredients to a large saucepan and cover with 2 litres cold water. Bring slowly up to the boil, skimming off any scum that forms on the surface. Simmer gently, uncovered, for 30 minutes, then strain through a fine sieve into a clean pan and simmer for a further 20–30 minutes to reduce and concentrate the flavour. Use as required, or cool and store in a covered container in the fridge and use within 2 days. The stock can be frozen for up to 1 month (see page 8 for more guidance on freezing).

# Tom Yam Soup

**Despite the long list of ingredients, this delicious soup is really quick to make. I would really recommend making your own nam prik pao paste, as the taste will be far superior to the ready-made stuff, and all the ingredients are easily found in Asian supermarkets or grocers. The paste keeps well in a sealed jar in the fridge for up to 3 months and is an excellent hot paste to liven up many a dish – my favourite being to thinly smear it in a fried egg sarnie!**

**Serves 4–6 | Takes 10 minutes to make, plus 15 minutes to make the nam prik pao paste, 5 minutes to cook the soup**

**For the nam prik pao paste**
**25g dried whole red chillies (Kashmiri, if possible)**
**3 tbsp sunflower oil**
**1 tbsp dried shrimps**
**3 cloves garlic, finely sliced**
**2 shallots, finely sliced**
**1 tsp shrimp paste**
**1 tbsp tamarind paste**
**1 tbsp jaggery (raw cane sugar) or light soft brown sugar**
**1 tbsp fish sauce (nam pla)**

**For the soup**
**1 litre chicken or vegetable stock**
**6 frozen or dried kaffir lime leaves**
**2 fresh red birdseye chillies, deseeded and finely chopped**
**200g shallots, chopped**
**4 cloves garlic, chopped**
**50g fresh galangal or fresh root ginger, peeled and finely sliced**
**3 lemongrass stalks, finely chopped**
**3 tbsp nam prik pao paste (ready-made, or see above)**
**4 tbsp fish sauce (nam pla)**
**2 tsp jaggery (raw cane sugar) or light soft brown sugar**
**juice of 2 limes**
**200g oyster mushrooms, sliced**
**4 tomatoes, chopped**
**4 spring onions, finely sliced**
**generous handful of fresh coriander leaves, chopped**

First, make the nam prik pao paste. Dry-fry the whole chillies in a wok over a medium heat until they darken slightly, then tip them into a spice mill and grind to a fine powder.

Add the oil to the wok and stir-fry the dried shrimps over a medium heat until they colour slightly, then remove with a slotted spoon and transfer to a food processor. Add the garlic to the oil in the wok and stir-fry until golden. Remove with a slotted spoon and add to the food processor. Stir-fry the shallots in the oil until they are also golden, then remove the wok from the heat and add the shallots to the food processor, along with the cooking oil left in the pan.

Add the ground chilli powder, shrimp paste, tamarind paste, jaggery, fish sauce and 3 tablespoons of cold water to the food processor and whizz everything together until you have a smooth paste. Transfer the paste back into the wok and heat gently for 2–3 minutes or until it is thick and jam-like. Transfer the paste to a clean jar and seal, then cool and store in the fridge for up to 3 months.

To make the soup, put the stock in a large saucepan, add the lime leaves and chillies and bring up to a gentle simmer.

Meanwhile, in a food processor, whizz together the shallots, garlic, galangal and lemongrass until you have a coarse paste. Add the paste to the hot stock and simmer, uncovered, for a couple of minutes. Add the nam prik pao paste, fish sauce, jaggery and lime juice, along with the mushrooms and tomatoes and simmer, uncovered, for 2–3 minutes or until the mushrooms are tender.

Remove the pan from the heat and remove and discard the lime leaves. Stir through the spring onions and chopped coriander and serve immediately in bowls.

**Not suitable for freezing.**

# Fennel, Lemon and Herb Soup with Haloumi 'Croûtons'

It's really worth making your own vegetable stock (see page 15) for this light and zesty soup, as the flavour is really central to the dish. I love grilled Haloumi cheese – its chewy, squeaky texture is oddly addictive, and its mild flavour makes it great for tossing in your favourite olive oil. Serve this soup with warm crusty ciabatta bread for a summery lunch.

Serves 4–6 | Takes 15 minutes to make, plus 1 hour cooking the broth, 10–15 minutes to cook the soup

**For the vegetable broth**
2 carrots, cut into chunks
2 sticks celery, cut into chunks
1 onion, cut into wedges
2 wide pared strips of lemon peel
1 tsp black peppercorns
fennel trimmings and herb stems from the soup (see below)

**For the soup**
2 fennel bulbs, trimmed and thinly sliced (add any trimmings to the broth)
4 spring onions, sliced on the diagonal into 1cm pieces
2 cloves garlic, thinly sliced
small bunch each of fresh dill, fresh parsley and fresh mint, chopped (add stems to the broth)
juice of 1 lemon
salt and freshly ground black pepper
extra virgin olive oil, for drizzling

**For the Haloumi 'croûtons'**
a little olive oil, for cooking
1 pack of Haloumi cheese (about 250g), cut into 1cm-thick slices
1 long fresh red chilli, deseeded and finely chopped
2 tbsp extra virgin olive oil

First, make the vegetable broth. Put the carrots, celery and onion into a large stock-pot. Cover with 3 litres of cold water, then add the lemon peel, peppercorns and fennel trimmings and herb stalks. Bring up to the boil, then turn down the heat and simmer, uncovered, for 1 hour.

For the soup, carefully strain the broth into a clean saucepan and discard all the vegetables, herbs, etc. Add the sliced fennel, spring onions and garlic to the pan and bring back up to the boil, then reduce the heat and simmer gently, uncovered, for around 5–8 minutes or until the vegetables are tender. Remove from the heat, stir through the chopped herbs and lemon juice and season to taste with salt and freshly ground black pepper.

Whilst the soup is cooking, make the Haloumi 'croûtons'. Heat a griddle pan until it is really hot, then brush lightly with a little olive oil. Griddle the cheese slices for a couple of minutes on each side until they are crisp and golden. Remove the cheese from the pan and chop it into 1cm cubes, then quickly toss it with the red chilli and extra virgin olive oil.

Serve the soup in bowls with a generous drizzle of extra virgin olive oil and the Haloumi 'croûtons' sprinkled on top just before you eat.

**Not suitable for freezing.**

# Jamaican Carrot and Pumpkin Soup

**It's worth seeking out Scotch bonnet chillies for this quick, sunshine-coloured soup, as they have a rich, fruity fragrance that other chillies lack – luckily they are more readily available in the supermarkets these days. But beware, they are exceptionally hot, so I suggest wearing gloves to prepare them, and use them with caution.**

**Serves 4–6 | Takes 10 minutes to make, 15 minutes to cook**

**2 tbsp vegetable oil**
**1 onion, finely chopped**
**400g pumpkin, peeled, deseeded and chopped into 1–2cm cubes**
**300g carrots, thickly sliced**
**20g fresh root ginger, peeled and grated**
**2 cloves garlic, chopped**
**1 litre vegetable or chicken stock**
**3 sprigs of fresh thyme, leaves picked**
**1 tsp ground allspice**
**1/2–1 fresh Scotch bonnet chilli, deseeded and chopped**
**juice of 1 lime**
**salt, to taste**

Heat the oil in a large saucepan and gently fry the onion for 5 minutes or so until softened. Add the pumpkin, carrots, ginger and garlic and fry for a further minute or two.

Pour in the stock and stir through the thyme, allspice and chilli. Bring up to the boil, then lower the heat and simmer, uncovered, for about 15 minutes or until the vegetables are tender.

Use a stick blender in the pan to part-purée the soup, leaving some lumps for texture. Finally, squeeze in the lime juice and season to taste with a little salt. You will probably not need any black pepper because the chilli is so fiery. Serve immediately.

**This soup freezes really well – freeze for up to 3 months. Defrost thoroughly, then reheat gently until piping hot. See page 8 for more guidance on this.**

# Rasam

This is a great soup for 'under-the-weather' days. The fact that the other name for this soup is 'South Indian pepper water' should give you a few clues as to what you can expect. Highly soothing, and a great cold beater, this soup is thin, brothy and very, very hot – you can literally feel it busting the bugs as you slurp. It uses an unusual spice, asafoetida, which is a natural flavour enhancer made from the ground root of a fennel-like plant. Don't be put off by its pungent smell when raw – once cooked, it has a mellow, slightly leek-like flavour. You can generally buy it in the spices section of supermarkets or visit an Asian supermarket and stock up on lots of other spicy treats at the same time.

**Serves 4–6 | Takes 10 minutes to make, 15 minutes to cook**

2 tbsp vegetable oil
2–6 hot dried whole red chillies, or to taste
1 tsp cumin seeds, roughly crushed
1 tsp black peppercorns, roughly crushed
1 tsp mustard seeds
$\frac{1}{2}$ tsp ground turmeric
3 fat cloves garlic, crushed
2–3 sprigs of fresh (or dried) curry leaves (optional)
500g passata (sieved/puréed tomatoes)
salt, to taste
small bunch of fresh coriander, leaves roughly chopped, to garnish

Heat the oil in a large saucepan and fry the chillies over a high heat until they start to crisp and darken. Add the crushed cumin and peppercorns, the mustard seeds, turmeric and garlic and fry for a further minute. Add the curry leaves if you are using them, but don't be tempted to replace them with curry powder as they are very different – simply leave them out if you can't get any.

Pour in the passata and then add 500ml cold water. Bring up to the boil, then lower the heat and simmer gently, uncovered, for 15 minutes. The soup should be fairly thin, so add a little more water if it is too thick. Season to taste with a little salt. Remove and discard the whole red chillies.

Serve the hot soup in bowls, garnished with a sprinkling of chopped coriander.

**This soup freezes well (without the coriander garnish) – freeze for up to 3 months. Defrost thoroughly, then reheat gently until piping hot. See page 8 for more guidance on this.**

# Five Spice Beef and Pea Soup

**An unauthentic but delicious Chinese version of the Vietnamese Pho recipe on page 45. For this clear soup, you could use the recipe for beef broth that forms the base of the Pho. Alternatively, use a good quality ready-made beef stock.**

**Serves 4–6 | Takes 10 minutes to make, plus 2 hours (or overnight) marinating, 10 minutes to cook**

**2 tsp Chinese five spice powder**
**1 tsp Sichuan peppercorns, roughly crushed**
**2 cloves garlic, crushed**
**3 tbsp vegetable oil**
**450g piece of beef fillet**
**a bunch of spring onions, finely sliced**
**300g frozen peas (no need to defrost)**
**2 star anise**
**1 litre beef stock (either homemade or good quality ready-made)**
**2 tbsp dark soy sauce**
**salt and freshly ground black pepper**

In a small bowl, mix together the five spice powder, crushed Sichuan peppercorns, garlic and 1 tablespoon of oil to make a paste. Rub this paste all over the beef fillet, then place in a dish, cover with cling film and leave to marinate in the fridge for at least 2 hours – overnight would be even better, if you have time.

Once you are ready to make the soup, heat another 1 tablespoon of oil in a large saucepan and gently fry the spring onions for a couple of minutes until they are just starting to soften. Add the frozen peas and star anise, then pour over the stock. Bring up to the boil, then lower the heat and simmer gently, uncovered, for 10 minutes.

Whilst the soup is simmering, add the remaining oil to a frying pan and heat until it is smoking hot. Quickly sear the beef fillet on all sides over as high a heat as possible. You are looking to caramelise the outside whilst still keeping it a little rare in the centre. Remove the beef to a plate and leave it to rest, covered loosely with foil, while you finish the soup.

Add the soy sauce to the soup and taste, adding a little salt and freshly ground black pepper, if necessary. Turn off the heat and cover the pan with a lid to keep the soup hot.

Slice the beef as thinly as possible and divide it between deep serving bowls. Pour over the soup and serve immediately.

**Not suitable for freezing.**

# Pork and Spring Onion Wonton Soup

**Wontons are little Chinese dumplings stuffed with meat or seafood that are usually cooked by floating them in a light chicken or vegetable broth. The filled dumplings are a bit fiddly and time-consuming to make, but they are well worth the effort when you taste the delicious end result. As a bit of a chilli addict, I like to serve this soup scattered with some fresh red chilli to add a bit of fresh zingy heat. Feel free to leave this out if you would prefer an altogether calmer soup.**

**Wonton wrappers are readily available in Asian food shops, usually in the freezer section (occasionally, they are available fresh).**

**Serves 4–6 | Takes 25 minutes to make, plus 30 minutes chilling, about 16–18 minutes to cook**

**For the wonton stuffing**
**500g minced pork**
**a bunch of spring onions, finely chopped**
**3cm piece of fresh root ginger, peeled and finely grated**
**2 cloves garlic, crushed**
**2 tbsp dark soy sauce**
**1 tbsp rice wine or dry sherry**
**1 tbsp toasted sesame oil**
**salt and freshly ground black pepper**

**200g pack frozen (defrosted) or fresh wonton wrappers (around 40 wrappers)**
**1 egg, lightly beaten**

**For the broth**
**1 litre chicken or vegetable stock (ideally homemade)**
**6 dried shiitake mushrooms, roughly chopped**
**2 star anise**
**4 heads of pak choi, or other oriental greens, roughly chopped**

**For the garnishes**
**3 spring onions, sliced**
**1–2 medium-hot fresh red chillies, deseeded and finely sliced (optional)**
**small handful of fresh coriander leaves**
**1 tbsp toasted sesame oil**

Make the wonton stuffing by mixing all the ingredients together in a bowl, seasoning generously with salt and freshly ground black pepper. Cover and set aside in the fridge for 30 minutes – longer if you have time – to allow the flavours to mingle.

When you are ready to make the dumplings, take a wonton wrapper and brush it lightly with beaten egg. Place a heaped teaspoon of the stuffing mixture in the middle of the wonton wrapper and draw up the sides, twisting them together to make a little sealed purse. Set aside and repeat with the remaining wonton wrappers and stuffing mixture.

Make the broth by bringing the stock up to the boil in a large saucepan. Add the dried mushrooms and star anise, then reduce the heat, cover and simmer gently for 10 minutes.

Stir through the pak choi, then add the wonton dumplings on top. Re-cover with a lid and simmer steadily for 6–8 minutes or until the wontons are cooked through.

Serve the hot broth in deep bowls with the wontons floating on top. To garnish, scatter over the spring onions, chillies and coriander leaves, then drizzle over a little sesame oil.

**Not suitable for freezing.**

# Quick Chicken Noodle Broth

**Healthy and super-quick, this is just the soup you need when you want something on the table in a flash. As it uses cooked chicken, I think of this as a good recipe for a Monday evening, making the most of the leftovers from Sunday's roast. You don't need to be too rigid about the vegetables you use either, just add them in the order they will take to cook so they stay a little crisp. I like to use a tiny bit of cornflour to thicken this soup ever so slightly, but simply leave it out, if you prefer.**

**Serves 4–6 | Takes 5 minutes to make, 5–10 minutes to cook**

**1 litre chicken or vegetable stock**
**2 tbsp dark soy sauce**
**1 tbsp rice vinegar**
**1 tbsp toasted sesame oil**
**4 generous handfuls of chopped vegetables (such as sliced carrots, sliced peppers, roughly torn fresh spinach or pak choi, shredded cabbage, sliced mushrooms, beansprouts, canned sweetcorn kernels)**
**200g cooked skinless, boneless chicken breast, cut into strips**
**2 blocks of dried egg noodles (about 150g in total)**
**1 tsp cornflour, mixed to a paste with a little cold water**
**salt and freshly ground black pepper**
**2 medium-hot fresh red chillies, deseeded and finely sliced, plus a bunch of spring onions, finely sliced, to garnish**

Pour the stock into a large saucepan and bring up to the boil. Season with the soy sauce, rice vinegar and oil.

Add the vegetables to the stock, one at a time, depending on the selection you are using, starting with the ones that take the longest to cook (for example, carrots and peppers will take a few minutes longer to cook than spinach, pak choi, cabbage, mushrooms or beansprouts; canned sweetcorn just needs heating through). Bring up to the boil, then lower the heat and simmer, uncovered, until the vegetables are tender.

Add the chicken and noodles, stirring until the noodles separate, then simmer for a further few minutes or until cooked.

If you are thickening the soup with cornflour, stir the cornflour paste through and simmer for a minute or two. Season to taste with a little salt and freshly ground black pepper.

Serve immediately, with the chillies and spring onions scattered over to garnish.

**Not suitable for freezing.**

# Goan Curried Fish Soup

In this creamy fish soup from southern India, two slightly unusual ingredients are used to give it a delicious and distinctive sweet and sour taste. Tamarind paste is made from the crushed pods of the tamarind tree and can be easily found in Asian food shops and some supermarkets. Jaggery is unrefined or raw cane sugar and can be a little harder to find in supermarkets, so substitute light soft brown sugar, if necessary.

**Serves 4–6 | Takes 15 minutes to make, 10 minutes to cook**

1 large onion, roughly chopped
4cm piece of fresh root ginger, peeled and roughly chopped
4 fat cloves garlic, roughly chopped
2 tbsp vegetable oil
1 tbsp cumin seeds
1 tbsp coriander seeds
1 tbsp mustard seeds
1 cinnamon stick
$^{1}/_{2}$ tsp ground turmeric
2 fresh green chillies, deseeded and chopped
3 tomatoes, chopped
600ml fish stock
400ml can coconut milk
1 tbsp tamarind paste, or the juice of $^{1}/_{2}$–1 lemon
2 tsp jaggery (raw cane sugar) or light soft brown sugar
600g skinless firm white fish fillets (such as haddock or cod), cut into bite-sized pieces
salt and freshly ground black pepper
2 tbsp unsweetened desiccated coconut and fresh coriander leaves, to garnish

Put the onion, ginger and garlic into a food processor and pulse until you have a coarse paste. If it is not coming together as a paste, add a tablespoon or so of cold water to help it along. Heat the oil in a large, heavy-based saucepan and gently fry the onion paste for 5 minutes to soften it a little.

Meanwhile, in a small frying pan, dry-fry the cumin, coriander and mustard seeds for a minute. As soon as you smell their aroma wafting up from the pan, tip them into a pestle and mortar and grind roughly.

Add the ground seeds to the onion paste, along with the cinnamon stick, turmeric and chillies. Fry for a further couple of minutes. Add the tomatoes, stock and coconut milk, then bring up to a gentle simmer and cook, uncovered, for 5 minutes.

Stir through the tamarind paste and jaggery and taste – it should be a nice balance of sweet and sour, so add a little more tamarind paste and/or jaggery, if necessary. Season to taste with salt and freshly ground black pepper. Finally, add the fish, stirring carefully so it is submerged beneath the liquid. Simmer for a few minutes or until the fish is just cooked through.

Serve the hot soup in bowls, garnished with a scattering of desiccated coconut and a few coriander leaves.

**This soup is suitable for freezing, but if you want to freeze it, it is best to do so before adding the fish (you can freeze the soup with the fish in, but the fish will break up on reheating). Freeze the soup for up to 3 months. Defrost the soup thoroughly, then reheat it gently until piping hot. See page 8 for more guidance on this. Add the raw fish to the reheated soup and cook as directed above, then serve with the garnishes.**

# HUMBLE

A bowl of soup can easily be the most economical thing you cook all week. With a few simple vegetables, some dried pulses, a few odds and sods lurking in the back of the fridge, you can create a meal whose frugality is far outweighed by its deliciousness. This kind of cooking, using just a handful of cheap ingredients, gives us a great sense of wellbeing through its humble simplicity.

# Beetroot Soup with Goat's Cheese Croûtons

**This quick soup takes advantage of those vacuum-packed ready-cooked beetroot that are so cheap in the supermarket. Just be sure to get the ones that are not packed in vinegar.**

**Serves 4–6 | Takes 10 minutes to make, 15 minutes to cook**

**For the soup**
**1 large onion, diced**
**2 tbsp olive oil**
**1 clove garlic, crushed**
**500g cooked beetroot (about 2 vacuum packs), cut into chunks**
**1 litre vegetable stock**
**1 tbsp balsamic vinegar**

**For the croûtons**
**4–6 slices of French baguette**
**olive oil, for brushing and drizzling**
**1 clove garlic, cut in half**
**1 small goat's cheese log (about 125g), cut into 4–6 rounds**
**a few fresh sage leaves, finely sliced**

Preheat the oven to 200°C/gas 6.

Make the soup. In a large saucepan, sweat the onion gently in the oil until it softens – this will take around 10 minutes, but be careful not to burn the onions or colour them too much, you are not trying to caramelise them.

Whilst the onions are cooking, start the croûtons. Brush the bread slices on both sides with oil, place them on a baking sheet and bake in the oven for 10 minutes or until they are crisp and dry. Remove from the oven.

When the onions are soft, add the garlic to the pan and fry gently for a further minute, then add the beetroot, stock and balsamic vinegar. Bring to the boil and simmer for a couple of minutes.

Purée the soup until it is really smooth, either using a stick blender in the pan, or carefully transfer the soup to a blender and purée, then return to the pan and reheat gently until hot, keeping the soup hot whilst you finish the croûtons.

Rub the garlic clove over one side of the crisp bread slices and top each slice with a round of goat's cheese. Sprinkle over the sliced sage leaves and finish with a drizzle of olive oil. Return to the oven for a few minutes until the cheese begins to melt.

Pour the hot soup into bowls and float a croûton on top of each portion. Serve immediately.

**This soup freezes well (without the croûtons) – freeze for up to 3 months. Defrost thoroughly, then reheat gently until piping hot. See page 8 for more guidance on this. Croûtons not suitable for freezing, so make these just before serving.**

# Creamy Pea and Mint Soup

I adore peas, they really are one of my all-time favourite things to eat, which in our house tends to bring me a lot of teasing along the lines of John Major's Spitting Image character: 'Nice peas Norma...'. Never mind, I roll with it. Peas freeze exceptionally well, and dare I say it, I almost prefer the frozen ones to the fresh ones, unless I have grown them myself, of course. This recipe is so simple and can be knocked up in a flash. And as you have cooked the peas, they are safe to re-freeze, meaning it's a good soup for batch cooking too.

**Serves 4–6 | Takes 15 minutes to make, 8 minutes to cook**

**25g unsalted butter**
**1 large onion, finely chopped**
**1 clove garlic, chopped**
**750g frozen peas (no need to defrost)**
**1 litre vegetable stock**
**small bunch of fresh mint, leaves picked and roughly chopped, plus extra to garnish**
**125ml single cream**
**salt and freshly ground black pepper**

Melt the butter in a heavy-based saucepan over a low heat. Gently sweat the onion for around 10 minutes or until it has softened but not coloured. Add the garlic and fry for a further minute before tipping in the frozen peas.

Pour in the stock and add the chopped mint leaves. Bring up to the boil, then reduce the heat and simmer gently, uncovered, for around 5–8 minutes or until both the onion and the peas are soft.

Purée the soup until smooth, either using a stick blender in the pan, or carefully transfer the soup to a blender and purée until smooth, then return to the pan.

Finally, add the cream, reheat gently and season to taste with salt and freshly ground black pepper. Serve with a little extra chopped mint to garnish.

**This soup freezes well – freeze for up to 3 months. Defrost thoroughly, then reheat gently until piping hot. See page 8 for more guidance on this.**

# Smoky Plum Tomato Soup

**This is a really simple soup using a ubiquitous store cupboard standby, canned tomatoes. Canned tomatoes can be rather plain, but they are livened up wonderfully by the addition of Spanish smoked paprika, another very useful ingredient to have lurking in the back of the spice cupboard. If you have a little parsley that needs using up, it makes a tasty fresh garnish; if you don't, not to worry as it will still taste great.**

**Serves 4–6 | Takes 10 minutes to make, 10 minutes to cook**

**2 tbsp olive oil
1 large onion, finely chopped
1 tsp Spanish smoked paprika (piquant or sweet)
2 cloves garlic, crushed
2 x 400g cans chopped tomatoes
1 tsp granulated sugar
salt and freshly ground black pepper
roughly chopped fresh flat-leaf parsley, to garnish (optional)**

Heat the oil in a heavy-based saucepan over a low heat and sweat the onion with the smoked paprika until soft. Add the garlic and cook for a further minute, taking care not to let it burn, otherwise it will turn bitter and unpleasant.

Pour in the tomatoes, add 500ml cold water and stir through the sugar. Bring up to the boil, then lower the heat and simmer gently, uncovered, for 10 minutes to thicken and concentrate the soup slightly.

Purée the soup to the desired consistency, either using a stick blender in the pan, or carefully transfer the soup to a blender and purée, then return to the pan and reheat gently until hot. As this is a rustic kind of soup, I prefer to use a stick blender so I have more control over the texture – blenders tend to take it one stage too smooth for my liking.

Season the soup with salt and freshly ground black pepper to taste and serve scattered with a little chopped parsley, if you like.

**This soup freezes well – freeze for up to 3 months. Defrost thoroughly, then reheat gently until piping hot. See page 8 for more guidance on this.**

**Cook's Tip**
If you carry on cooking this soup at a gentle simmer until it thickens and reduces, it makes a wonderful piquant pasta sauce, or a lively tomato sauce base for a homemade pizza. Make a double or even treble batch and freeze it in portions for a day when cooking is the last thing on your mind.

# White Bean Soup with Wild Garlic Pesto

**This is perhaps the humblest of humble soups, using exceptionally economical dried beans and totally free wild garlic foraged from the woods. I would urge you to try and get hold of wild garlic when it is in season (March–May), as it is really commonly found in woodland and it feels good to go back to our hunter-gatherer roots. If you can't find any, substitute with a garlicky basil pesto, although the soup will no longer be quite so frugal!**

**Serves 4–6 | Takes 10 minutes to make, plus overnight soaking of the beans, 55 minutes to cook**

**300g dried white beans (such as white kidney or cannellini beans), soaked overnight in cold water, drained and rinsed**
**3 tbsp olive oil**
**2 leeks, washed and finely chopped**
**2 cloves garlic, crushed**
**a sprig of fresh rosemary, needles picked and finely chopped**
**2 litres vegetable stock**

**For the wild garlic pesto**
**60g pine nuts**
**2 handfuls of wild garlic leaves, well washed and roughly chopped**
**4–6 tbsp olive oil**
**3 tbsp finely grated fresh Parmesan cheese**
**salt and freshly ground black pepper**

Heat the oil in a large, heavy-based saucepan and gently sweat the leeks with the garlic and rosemary until they soften slightly. Take care not to brown them at all or they will take on a bitter taste.

Add the drained beans and stock, bring up to the boil and boil rapidly for 10 minutes. Turn the heat down to a steady simmer and carry on cooking, uncovered, until the beans are meltingly soft – this will take about 45 minutes.

Whilst the soup is cooking, make the pesto. Toast the pine nuts in a dry frying pan until golden brown, then tip them into a food processor. Add the wild garlic, oil and Parmesan and whizz until you have a smooth paste. Season to taste with salt and freshly ground black pepper. Set aside.

When the beans are soft, carefully pour the soup into a blender and purée until smooth, adding a little more water if it is too thick. Return to the pan and reheat gently until hot. Check the seasoning, adding a little salt and freshly ground black pepper to taste.

Serve the hot soup in deep bowls with the pesto drizzled on top.

**Not suitable for freezing.**

# Curried Parsnip and Apple Soup

In the cooler months, I often have a few parsnips lurking in the bottom of the fridge, a result of over-enthusiastic shopping for a roast dinner, and soup is a great way of using them up. Parsnips make lovely smooth-textured soups and their sweet flavour is classic when teamed with sharp Bramley apples and the merest hint of curry powder. Sometimes I add a little cream if I happen to have some that needs using up.

**Serves 4–6 | Takes 15 minutes to make, 15 minutes to cook**

1 tbsp vegetable oil
1 large onion, chopped
2 cloves garlic, chopped
600g parsnips, chopped
1 Bramley cooking apple, peeled, cored and roughly chopped
1 tbsp medium curry powder or curry paste
1 litre vegetable stock
3 tbsp double cream (optional)
salt and freshly ground black pepper

Heat the oil in a large, heavy-based frying pan and gently fry the onion for about 15 minutes or until soft and golden brown.

Add the garlic, parsnips, apple and curry powder. Fry for a further couple of minutes before pouring over the stock. Bring up to a steady simmer and cook gently, uncovered, for another 15 minutes or so until the parsnips are soft.

Carefully pour the soup into a blender and purée until really smooth. Return to the pan and add the cream, if using, and a splash more water if it is slightly too thick. Reheat gently, then season to taste with salt and freshly ground black pepper.

Serve immediately, perhaps with some warm naan bread.

**This soup freezes really well – freeze for up to 3 months. Defrost thoroughly, then reheat gently until piping hot. See page 8 for more guidance on this.**

# Spinach and Nutmeg Soup

**Frozen spinach is so easy to use and cheaper than the fresh stuff, so I often have some lurking in the freezer for adding to soups or risottos. This delicious soup, with its vivid green hue, exudes health and wholesomeness and tastes great too. Like many of the milk-based soups in this book, I like to thicken it with a little flour – it just seems to hold the whole thing together, creating a more cohesive texture, which I like.**

**Serves 4–6 | Takes 5 minutes to make, 10–15 minutes to cook**

25g unsalted butter
1 tbsp olive oil
1 onion, finely chopped
1 clove garlic, crushed
500g frozen blocks of spinach (no need to defrost)
1 litre milk (or half milk, half cold water, if you prefer)
$\frac{1}{2}$ nutmeg, freshly grated, or to taste
1 tbsp plain flour
salt and freshly ground black pepper
a little single cream, to serve (optional)

Melt the butter with the oil in a large saucepan. Gently sweat the onion and garlic for a few minutes until slightly softened.

Add the blocks of frozen spinach and pour over the milk. Grate over the nutmeg to taste and season with a little salt and plenty of freshly ground black pepper. Bring up to the boil, then lower the heat and simmer, uncovered, for around 5–8 minutes, stirring from time to time to break up the spinach as it defrosts.

Once the spinach has broken up, carefully transfer the soup to a blender and add the flour. Purée until completely smooth, then return to the pan, reheat gently and simmer until thickened, stirring all the time.

Serve hot in bowls with a swirl of cream, if you have some.

**This soup freezes well – freeze for up to 3 months. Defrost thoroughly, then reheat gently until piping hot. See page 8 for more guidance on this.**

# Cream of Celery Soup

This is another soup I remember my mum making when I was young. Celery is one of those things you either love or hate. I love it, though I have no idea how mum got me to eat it as a child – my kids grimace in agony at the mere suggestion of it! The gorgeous strong celery flavour in this soup is tempered and softened by cooking it in creamy milk. This is one of the few soups that I sieve before serving as celery can be annoyingly stringy and I think it's worth the extra effort involved. Super-humble it may be, but I see no reason not to take a little care to make it great.

**Serves 4–6 | Takes 10 minutes to make, 20 minutes to cook**

**25g unsalted butter**
**1 tbsp olive oil**
**1 head of celery, trimmed and sliced**
**2 cloves garlic, crushed**
**600ml milk**
**2 tbsp plain flour**
**salt and freshly ground black pepper**
**120g mature Cheddar cheese, grated, to serve**

Melt the butter with the oil in a large saucepan, add the celery and gently sweat over a low heat for about 5 minutes or until slightly softened, then add the garlic and cook for a further minute.

Pour in the milk and 600ml cold water, bring up to a steady simmer and cook, uncovered, for 15–20 minutes or until the celery is completely soft.

Carefully transfer the soup to a blender, add the flour and purée until really smooth. Return to the pan, bring back to the boil and cook for 5 minutes, stirring as the soup thickens. Pass the soup through a sieve into a clean pan and season with salt and freshly ground black pepper.

Reheat gently until hot, then serve in bowls, sprinkled with some grated cheese.

**This soup freezes well (without the cheese) – freeze for up to 3 months. Defrost thoroughly, then reheat gently until piping hot. See page 8 for more guidance on this.**

# Leek and Potato Soup

A complete classic, leek and potato soup is so cheap, simple and satisfying. I like to use a stick blender in the pan to purée this soup just a little, leaving plenty of lumps of vegetables, as I like the texture. Feel free to purée the lot if you prefer a smooth soup, or even leave it totally unblended if you want a rustic version. This soup freezes really well, so it's a good recipe for batch cooking on a wet and windy autumn day.

**Serves 4–6 | Takes 10 minutes to make, 20 minutes to cook**

**50g unsalted butter**
**4 large leeks, washed and cut into 1cm pieces**
**1 onion, finely chopped**
**2 large potatoes, cut into 1cm cubes**
**1 litre chicken or vegetable stock**
**2 tsp dried mixed herbs (such as herbes de Provence)**
**salt and freshly ground black pepper**
**a little single cream or crème fraîche and a few snipped fresh chives, to garnish (optional)**

Melt the butter gently in a large, heavy-based saucepan and sweat the leeks and onion over a low heat for a few minutes until slightly softened. Add the potatoes and pour over the stock, then bring up to a gentle simmer.

Add the herbs and season with a little salt and freshly ground black pepper and simmer, uncovered, until the leeks and potatoes are soft and tender. This should take around 15–20 minutes, depending on the size you cut your vegetables.

Purée the soup to the desired consistency, either using a stick blender in the pan, or carefully transfer the soup to a blender and purée, then return to the pan and reheat gently until hot. Serve.

This soup looks pretty garnished with a swirl of cream or crème fraîche and a scattering of snipped chives, but it tastes just as good without.

**This soup does freeze but if you have left it course-textured, the potatoes may disintegrate a little on reheating. This soup will freeze for up to 3 months. Defrost thoroughly, then reheat gently until piping hot. See page 8 for more guidance on this.**

# Creamy Sweetcorn and Rosemary Soup

**Rosemary and sweetcorn seem to be made for each other, the sharpness of one perfectly offsetting the sweetness of the other. Frozen sweetcorn is a great ingredient to have on standby and this wholesome soup can be knocked up in a matter of minutes. Teamed with some nice cheese and crusty bread, this soup makes a great impromptu lunch for friends.**

**Serves 4–6 | Takes 10 minutes to make, 10–15 minutes to cook**

**25g unsalted butter**
**1 onion, finely chopped**
**2 sprigs of fresh rosemary, needles picked and finely chopped**
**300g frozen sweetcorn kernels (no need to defrost)**
**500ml milk**
**500ml vegetable stock**
**1 tbsp plain flour**
**salt and freshly ground black pepper**

Melt the butter in a large saucepan and gently sweat the onion with the rosemary for 5 minutes or so until slightly softened.

Add the frozen sweetcorn kernels, pour over the milk and stock, bring up to the boil, then reduce the heat and simmer for 5–10 minutes or until the sweetcorn is cooked.

Carefully pour the soup into a blender, add the flour and purée until smooth. Return to the pan and bring to a steady simmer. Cook for a few minutes, stirring all the time, until the soup is thick and creamy.

Season with a little salt and plenty of freshly ground black pepper and serve.

**Not suitable for freezing.**

**Cook's Tip**
You can sieve this soup at the end of cooking, just before serving, if you prefer a completely smooth soup.

# Leftover Chicken and Pasta Soup

**A wonderful frugal and tasty soup for a Monday night supper, using the remnants of Sunday's roast chicken. I start off the stock before work on Monday morning, which is simply a question of bunging all the ingredients in a large pan, bringing up to a simmer, then cooking in a low oven all day. By the time you come home, your supper is halfway to being on the table.**

**Serves 4–6 | Takes 15 minutes to make, plus 8 hours cooking the stock, 20 minutes to cook the soup**

**For the stock**

**1 roast chicken carcass**
**2 onions, unpeeled and quartered**
**2 carrots, cut into chunks**
**stems of a small bunch of flat-leaf parsley, leaves reserved for the soup**
**1 tsp black peppercorns**
**2 bay leaves**
**1 sprig of fresh rosemary**

**For the soup**

**4 rashers smoked streaky bacon, cut into 1cm strips or dice**
**2 cloves garlic, crushed**
**leaves from a small bunch of flat-leaf parsley (see stock above), roughly chopped**
**250g dried small soup pasta (such as conchigliette, ditalini, orzo or small macaroni)**
**4 generous handfuls of mixed vegetables, chopped into bite-sized pieces (such as carrots, leeks, broccoli, celery, sweetcorn kernels)**
**salt and freshly ground black pepper**
**finely grated fresh Parmesan cheese, to serve (optional)**

Make the stock. Start by giving your chicken carcass a really thorough picking over and removing any meat. A large (2kg) chicken for a family of 4 should yield about 150–200g of leftover meat. As you pick off the meat, transfer the bits of skin, bones and fat into a large stock-pot, along with any jelly from the roasting tin. Once you have separated all the meat, put it in the fridge until you are ready to make the soup.

Add all the remaining stock ingredients to the stock-pot, together with 2 litres cold water, and bring up to the boil. Cover the pan with a tight-fitting lid or a double piece of foil. This will prevent too much evaporation. Transfer the pan to a very low oven (about 110°C/gas ¼ and cook for around 8 hours – even an hour or two longer won't harm. When the stock is cooked, strain it into a large bowl and discard the bones, vegetables and herbs. Set the stock aside.

Make the soup. Give the stock-pot a quick rinse, then add the bacon to the stock-pot and fry in its own fat until golden brown. Add the garlic and parsley, pour in the reserved stock and season with salt and freshly ground black pepper. Add the pasta and vegetables.

Bring up to the boil, then lower the heat and simmer, uncovered, until everything is tender. It's tricky to be precise here about cooking times as it will very much depend on the vegetables you are using. I don't think this is an occasion to serve either the vegetables or pasta too al dente – this is soup for comfort not crunch. Carrots and celery will take longest, about 15 minutes, then the pasta will take 8–10 minutes, depending on its size. More tender vegetables like sweetcorn kernels or broccoli need only have 5 minutes or so at the end. Serve the hot soup in bowls, sprinkled with a little grated Parmesan cheese, if you have some.

**Not suitable for freezing.**

# Broad Bean Soup with Tzatziki

I used to hate broad beans, but now I love them. The trick, for me, is getting rid of the tough outer skin to reveal the tender vivid green bean underneath – this is sometimes called double-podding and is admittedly a little fiddly but well worth it. This soup uses frozen broad beans, which are really versatile and fresh tasting. As this soup gets sieved after cooking, you only need to double-pod some extra beans for the garnish. The cool tzatziki makes a lovely contrast to the hot soup, making this the perfect dish for a summer's day lunch.

**Serves 4–6 | Takes 10 minutes to make, 15 minutes to cook**

1 onion, finely chopped
2 tbsp olive oil
1 clove garlic, crushed
800g frozen broad beans (no need to defrost)
1 litre vegetable stock
2 sprigs of fresh mint
salt and freshly ground black pepper
200g frozen broad beans, to garnish

**For the tzatziki**
$1/2$ cucumber, coarsely grated
1 clove garlic, crushed
250ml tub natural Greek-style yogurt
handful of fresh mint leaves, finely chopped

In a heavy-based saucepan, gently sweat the onion in the oil for around 5–10 minutes or until soft. Add the garlic and cook for a further minute, then add the broad beans and pour over the stock.

Add the mint sprigs, stems and all, and bring the soup up to a gentle simmer. Cook, uncovered, for 10 minutes, by which time the broad beans should be soft. Fish out the mint stalks and discard.

Carefully transfer the soup to a blender and purée until smooth, then pass through a sieve back into the saucepan to get rid of the tough bits of skin. Bring back to a simmer and season to taste with salt and freshly ground black pepper.

Meanwhile, cook the broad beans for the garnish. Simmer the broad beans in a small pan of boiling water for a few minutes or until just tender. Drain and cool slightly, then squeeze them out of their pods (discarding the pods) and set aside.

To make the tzatziki, combine all the ingredients in a small bowl and season to taste with salt and freshly ground black pepper.

Serve the hot soup with a generous dollop of tzatziki on top of each portion, and garnish with a scattering of the extra broad beans.

**This soup freezes well (without the tzatziki) – freeze for up to 3 months. Defrost thoroughly, then reheat gently until piping hot. See page 8 for more guidance on this. Tzatziki is not suitable for freezing, so make this just before serving.**

# Moorish Chickpea Soup

Dried chickpeas, like all dried pulses, are incredible value for money and are really good for you. The only downside is that you have to remember to soak them overnight, but I think such forethought is a small price to pay for the delicious spicy soup you are rewarded with. This tasty soup is perfect and warming for slightly chilly days.

**Serves 4–6 | Takes 15 minutes to make, plus overnight soaking of the chickpeas, 50 minutes to cook**

400g dried chickpeas, soaked
  overnight in cold water, drained
  and rinsed
2 large onions, chopped
2 tbsp olive oil
2 cloves garlic, crushed
2 tsp cumin seeds, roughly ground
2 tsp dried oregano
1 tsp Spanish smoked paprika
2 litres chicken or vegetable stock
salt and freshly ground black
  pepper
chopped fresh flat-leaf parsley
  and extra Spanish smoked
  paprika, to garnish
extra virgin olive oil, for drizzling

In a large, heavy-based saucepan, fry the onions in the olive oil for about 10–15 minutes or until golden and caramelised.

Add the garlic, cumin, oregano and smoked paprika and fry for a further minute or so before adding the drained chickpeas.

Pour over the stock, bring up to the boil and boil rapidly for 10 minutes. Turn the heat down and simmer, uncovered, for about 45–50 minutes or until the chickpeas are soft.

Using a stick blender in the pan, purée the soup so you have a reasonably smooth texture with plenty of whole chickpeas. Taste, then season generously with salt and freshly ground black pepper.

Serve each portion garnished with a little chopped parsley and a sprinkle of paprika, and finish with a good drizzle of extra virgin olive oil.

**Not suitable for freezing.**

# Cream of Celeriac Soup

**Celeriac is such a valuable vegetable – underneath its ugly gnarled skin it has an interesting celery-like flavour and delicate soft texture when cooked. It makes a great cheap soup – a little goes a long way in the taste department – when bulked up with the humble potato. The one drawback with celeriac is that once it is peeled it browns very quickly, so either peel and chop it moments before adding it to the pan or prepare it and store in water with a generous squeeze of lemon juice to stop the oxidation process.**

**Serves 4–6 | Takes 10 minutes to make, 15 minutes to cook**

**50g unsalted butter**
**2 onions, chopped**
**2 potatoes, chopped**
**1 large celeriac, chopped**
**2 tsp dried sage**
**500ml milk**
**500ml vegetable stock**
**salt and freshly ground black
    pepper**

Melt the butter in a large saucepan over a low heat and gently fry the onions for about 10 minutes or until soft.

Add the potatoes, celeriac and sage, pour over the milk and stock and bring up to the boil. Turn the heat down and simmer steadily, uncovered, until the vegetables are cooked – this will take about 10–15 minutes, depending on the size you have cut the vegetables.

Carefully transfer the soup to a blender and purée until really smooth. Return to the pan and bring back to a gentle simmer. Taste and season with salt and freshly ground black pepper.

Serve hot with plenty of buttered crusty bread.

**This soup freezes really well – freeze for up to 3 months. Defrost thoroughly, then reheat gently until piping hot. See page 8 for more guidance on this.**

# Roasted Root Vegetable Soup

**I made this soup once with leftover roast vegetables from Sunday lunch. It was really good so I thought it was worth roasting the vegetables especially for soup. Here is the recipe – so simple, everything gets bunged in a tray in the oven to roast to a gorgeous caramel crispness, then you whizz it up with a little vegetable stock. A delicious and hearty soup that requires very minimal effort in the kitchen.**

**Serves 4–6 | Takes 30–40 minutes to make, 10 minutes to cook**

**2 large parsnips, cut into chunks**
**2 large potatoes, cut into chunks**
**2 carrots, cut into chunks**
**1 large onion, quartered**
**3 cloves garlic, unpeeled and bruised with the back of a knife**
**4 tbsp olive oil**
**6 fresh sage leaves**
**1 litre vegetable stock**
**salt and freshly ground black pepper**

Preheat the oven to 190°C/gas 5.

In a large roasting tin, toss all the vegetables and garlic in the oil until completely coated, then spread them out in an even layer in the tin. Tuck in the sage leaves and season with a little salt and freshly ground black pepper. Roast in the oven until soft and caramelised at the edges – this will take around 30–40 minutes, depending on the size you have cut your vegetables.

Remove from the oven and squeeze the garlic cloves out of their skins, discarding the skins. Tip everything into a blender, along with the stock, and purée until smooth.

Transfer the soup to a pan and bring up to a simmer, adding a little more stock or water if it is too thick. Taste to check the seasoning, adding a little more salt and black pepper, if necessary, and then serve.

**This soup freezes well – freeze for up to 3 months. Defrost thoroughly, then reheat gently until piping hot. See page 8 for more guidance on this.**

# Red Lentil Soup with Coriander Chutney

Based on the gorgeous Indian red lentil dhal, this soup is wholesome and spicy. The garnishes really lift the whole dish and are worth the extra effort to make, but if you are short of time or don't have the ingredients to hand, then a generous dollop of yogurt would be an alternative accompaniment.

**Serves 4–6 | Takes 15 minutes to make, 25 minutes to cook**

1 tbsp coriander seeds
2 tsp cumin seeds
1–2 tsp dried chilli flakes
1 tsp black peppercorns
1 large onion, roughly chopped
2 cloves garlic, chopped
2cm piece of fresh root ginger, peeled and roughly chopped
2 tbsp vegetable oil
1 tsp ground turmeric
300g dried red lentils
2 litres vegetable stock
salt, to taste

**For the coriander chutney**
small bunch of fresh coriander
juice of 1 lime
1 tbsp vegetable oil
1 fresh green chilli, deseeded and roughly chopped
1 clove garlic, crushed
1 tsp caster sugar

**For the crispy fried onions**
vegetable oil, for frying
1 large onion, finely sliced

In a large saucepan, dry-fry the coriander seeds, cumin seeds, chilli flakes and black peppercorns for about a minute until they are lightly toasted. As soon as you smell their aroma wafting up from the pan, tip the mixture into a pestle and mortar and roughly grind. Set aside.

Put the onion, garlic and ginger into a food processor and purée until you have a coarse paste, adding 1 or 2 tablespoons of cold water, if necessary, to help it purée. Pour the oil into the saucepan and fry the onion paste over a medium heat for about 5 minutes or until it is soft and translucent, stirring from time to time to prevent it sticking. Add the ground spices, plus the turmeric, and fry for a further minute or so before adding the lentils and stirring well to mix.

Add the stock, bring up to a simmer and cook, uncovered, for around 25 minutes or until the lentils are soft and collapsing. You may need to add a little more stock or water if the soup is too thick. Season to taste with salt.

Whilst the soup is cooking, prepare the garnishes. For the coriander chutney, place all the ingredients into a food processor and whizz until smooth. You are looking for a consistency that you can drizzle – a bit like a runny pesto – so add a splash of cold water, if necessary.

For the crispy fried onions, heat enough oil in a heavy-based frying pan so that the onion will be nearly covered. Fry the onion slices over a medium-high heat until they are golden and crispy. Remove with a slotted spoon and drain on several layers of kitchen paper.

Serve the hot soup in bowls with a sprinkling of onions and a drizzle of chutney on top of each portion.

**This soup freezes brilliantly (without the garnishes) – freeze for up to 3 months. Defrost thoroughly, then reheat gently until piping hot. See page 8 for more guidance on this. Garnishes not suitable for freezing, so make these just before serving.**

# Cream of White Onion Soup with Thyme

**Even when the cupboards are really bare there are usually a few things you can rely on having around. Onions, milk and a little flour are basically all you need to whip up this quick and comforting soup. I like to add some fresh thyme as it goes really well with onions and, unless it's the depths of winter, I can usually find some in the garden. Dried thyme would be a perfectly good alternative.**

**Serves 4–6 | Takes 10 minutes to make, 20 minutes to cook**

**50g unsalted butter**
**600g onions, roughly chopped**
**2–3 sprigs of fresh thyme or 1 tsp dried thyme**
**1 litre milk**
**2 tbsp plain flour**
**1 tbsp English mustard (either powder or ready-mixed paste)**
**salt and freshly ground black pepper**
**a little single cream, to serve (optional)**

Melt the butter in a large saucepan over a low heat and sweat the onions with the thyme for 5 minutes or until they are slightly softened. Pour in the milk, bring up to a gentle simmer and cook, uncovered, until the onions are soft and melting – this will take around 15 minutes. If you are using fresh thyme, fish out the stalks and discard.

Carefully pour the soup into a blender, add the flour and mustard and purée until smooth. Return to the pan and simmer steadily, stirring constantly, until the soup has thickened. Taste and season with salt and freshly ground black pepper.

Serve the hot soup in deep bowls with plenty of bread to dip in. If you have a little single cream lurking in the fridge, a little swirl on top will look pretty and enhance the silky texture, but not to worry if you don't – it will still taste lovely.

**This soup freezes really well – freeze for up to 3 months. Defrost thoroughly, then reheat gently until piping hot. See page 8 for more guidance on this.**

# Cream of Mushroom Soup

**Simple, cheap and delicious, I remember my mum making a mushroom soup very like this one when I was a child. I use large boxes of 'value' mushrooms from the supermarket, or the reduced, slightly past-their-best mushrooms. Of course you could use fancier and more interesting varieties, but I think that rather misses the point of this very quick and frugal soup. I like to eat this soup with homemade herby garlic bread, which is so much quicker, cheaper and more tasty than the shop-bought stuff. I have also included the recipe for this at the end.**

**Serves 4–6 | Takes 10 minutes to make, 10 minutes to cook, plus 15 minutes for the garlic bread**

**50g unsalted butter
800g mushrooms
2–3 cloves garlic, roughly chopped
2 tbsp plain flour
1 litre milk
salt and freshly ground black pepper**

Melt the butter in a large, heavy-based saucepan over a gentle heat.

Give the mushrooms a quick wipe over with kitchen paper to remove any soil, then tear roughly into pieces, stalks and all, and toss into the pan. Add the garlic and a generous pinch of salt and stir well to coat the mushrooms all over. Sweat the mushrooms over a low heat for around 10 minutes or until they are soft and wilted.

Add the flour to the pan and stir well to coat the mushrooms. Pour in the milk, stirring constantly to blend out any lumps of flour. Bring gently to the boil, then cook at a steady simmer for a good 5 minutes, stirring. It is important that this soup simmers quite rapidly to cook the flour thoroughly otherwise it may taste a bit 'floury'.

Purée the soup until smooth, either using a stick blender in the pan, or carefully transfer the soup to a blender and purée, then return to the pan and reheat gently until hot. Season to taste with salt and freshly ground black pepper and serve immediately with garlic bread.

**This soup freezes well – freeze for up to 3 months. Defrost thoroughly, then reheat gently until piping hot. See page 8 for more guidance on this.**

### Cook's Tip
To make Herby Garlic Bread, cut 2cm-thick slices partway through 1 small French stick. In a small bowl, beat 100g softened butter, 2 crushed cloves garlic, 1 teaspoon of dried mixed herbs (such as herbes de Provence) and salt and freshly ground black pepper together until well mixed. Spread the garlic butter liberally between the bread slices. Wrap the loaf loosely in foil and bake in a preheated oven at 180°C/gas 4 for about 15 minutes.

VEGETABLE

# White Gazpacho with Almonds and Garlic

**Otherwise known as Ajo Blanco, this classic Spanish soup is a pure white version of the more commonly known tomato gazpacho. It's a great recipe to make for a summer lunch with friends as it can be made several days in advance and chilled in the fridge – the flavour improves as it matures.**

*Serves 4–6 | Takes 5 minutes to make, plus soaking the bread, at least 2 hours to chill*

**100g good quality white bread, crusts removed**
**200g whole blanched almonds**
**3 cloves garlic, crushed**
**200ml good quality extra virgin olive oil (Spanish, if possible)**
**3–4 tbsp sherry vinegar**
**salt and freshly ground black pepper**
**handful of seedless green grapes, sliced in half, to garnish**
**a little good quality extra virgin olive oil, for drizzling**

Put the bread in a dish, add enough cold water to cover and leave to soak for 15 minutes.

Tip the almonds into a food processor and whizz until they are as finely ground as possible. Squeeze the water out of the bread, then add the bread to the processor along with the garlic and process until you have a smooth paste.

With the motor running, gradually pour in the olive oil until you have a smooth emulsion, then add enough cold water to give you the consistency of single cream. Add the sherry vinegar to taste and season with plenty of salt and freshly ground black pepper.

Pour the soup into a bowl, cover and chill in the fridge for a good 2 hours or more.

Serve the soup ice-cold, garnished with the grape halves and a drizzle of extra virgin olive oil on top of each portion.

**The soup is suitable for freezing (without the grape garnish) – freeze for up to 3 months. Defrost thoroughly before serving chilled. See page 8 for more guidance on this. Grape garnish not suitable for freezing, so simply add this and the olive oil drizzle just before serving.**

# Wild Nettle Soup

Very unusual, with a slightly spinachy taste, nettle soup is not something you will make everyday but I urge you to try it once, preferably in spring when the nettle leaves are new and fresh. The most time-consuming bit is picking the nettles themselves – don't even think about doing it without gloves!

**Serves 4–6 | Takes 10 minutes to make (plus nettle picking!), 15 minutes to cook**

**1 large onion, finely chopped**
**2 tbsp olive oil**
**1 clove garlic, crushed**
**2 potatoes, cut into 1cm cubes**
**3–4 large handfuls of nettle leaves (only use the new fresh leaves)**
**1 litre vegetable or chicken stock**
**salt and freshly ground black pepper**
**crème fraîche or sour cream, to serve**

Gently fry the onion in the oil in a large saucepan for 10 minutes or so until soft and lightly golden. Add the garlic and potatoes and fry for a further minute or so.

Whilst the onions are cooking, wash the nettle leaves really thoroughly, wearing gloves, and discard any that are discoloured. Shake the leaves dry in a colander and roughly chop, then add to the onion and potato mixture in the pan.

Pour over the stock and season with a little salt and freshly ground black pepper. Bring up to the boil, then lower the heat and simmer, uncovered, for around 10–12 minutes or until the potatoes are soft.

Carefully transfer the soup to a blender and purée until smooth. Return to the pan, bring back up to a simmer and taste to check the seasoning, adding a little more salt and black pepper, if necessary.

Serve hot with a swirl of crème fraîche or sour cream on top of each portion.

**This soup freezes really well. It is really only worth making in April and May when the nettles are young, so if you can face all that picking, it's worth making a double batch and freezing some. Freeze for up to 3 months. Defrost thoroughly, then reheat gently until piping hot. See page 8 for more guidance on this.**

VEGETABLE

# Spiced Cauliflower and Yogurt Soup with Caramelised Butter

**This is a really delicious soup, lightly spiced, thickened with rich yogurt and finished in traditional Turkish style with a drizzle of caramelised butter. I love cauliflower, it's cheap and nutritious and it's great to use it for something other than the traditional cauliflower cheese.**

*Serves 4–6 | Takes 10–15 minutes to make, 15–20 minutes to cook*

**2 tbsp coriander seeds**
**125g unsalted butter**
**1 large onion, finely chopped**
**2 tbsp dried chilli flakes**
**3 cloves garlic, crushed**
**1 large cauliflower, leaves and main stalk discarded, florets roughly chopped**
**1 litre vegetable stock**
**1 tbsp plain flour**
**250ml tub full-fat natural Greek-style yogurt**
**generous handful of fresh coriander, leaves roughly chopped**
**salt and freshly ground black pepper**
**a pinch of dried chilli flakes, to garnish**

In a large, heavy-based saucepan, dry-fry the coriander seeds for a minute or two until lightly toasted. Tip into a pestle and mortar and roughly grind.

Let the pan cool for a minute or two, then melt 50g of the butter over a low heat. Add the onion, ground coriander and chilli flakes and fry gently for around 10 minutes – the onion should be soft and lightly caramelised by this stage.

Add the garlic and fry for a further minute before adding the cauliflower and pouring over the stock. Bring up to the boil, then lower the heat and simmer, uncovered, for 15–20 minutes or until the cauliflower is really soft.

Carefully pour the soup into a blender and add the flour. Purée until smooth, then return to the pan, stir through the yogurt and bring gently up to a simmer. Cook for a few minutes to thicken the soup, stirring all the time. Stir through the chopped coriander and season to taste with salt and freshly ground black pepper.

Meanwhile, to make the caramelised butter, melt the remaining 75g butter in a small, heavy-based saucepan over a low heat. The butter should separate and gradually turn golden brown – this will take around 5 minutes, but take care to do this over a low heat as it easily burns.

Serve the soup in bowls with the caramelised butter drizzled over the top of each portion. Garnish with a few flakes of dried chilli.

**Not suitable for freezing.**

# GARDEN BOUNTY

One of the best things about making soup is their usefulness in using up seasonal gluts of vegetables, whether they are those that you have grown yourself, or the super-cheap bulk bags of veg from the shops. These recipes are all about celebrating the best of what's economical, fresh and glorious during their prime growing season.

# Broccoli and Toasted Almond Soup

This recipe gives you a lot of soup for not a lot of vegetables – the almonds seem to bulk it out and give it a really filling and rich texture. Toasting the almonds might seem like a bit of a faff but it really does enhance the nutty flavour – in fact it's a great trick for all types of nut, just a matter of a minute or two in a hot, dry pan will make all the difference to their flavour. The other great thing about this recipe is that it is completely dairy-free, making it a great choice for vegans or lactose-intolerant guests.

**Serves 4–6 | Takes 8 minutes to make, 10–15 minutes to cook**

**75g flaked almonds**
**2 tbsp olive oil**
**3 cloves garlic, crushed**
**600g broccoli (about 2 heads), chopped**
**1 litre good quality vegetable stock**
**salt and freshly ground black pepper**

Toast the almonds in a dry saucepan for a minute or two, shaking the pan from time to time to stop them burning. Add the oil and garlic to the pan and fry for literally a few seconds until you just smell the garlic aromas wafting up. The pan is already hot from toasting the almonds so take care not to burn the garlic.

Add the broccoli, toss quickly in the oil to coat it and then pour in the stock. Bring up to a steady simmer and cover with a lid so that the broccoli half-steams and half-simmers. Cook for 7–10 minutes or until the broccoli is tender but still has a little bite.

Carefully transfer the soup to a blender and purée until smooth, then return to the pan and reheat gently until hot.

Season to taste with salt and freshly ground black pepper – this soup has a subtle nutty flavour and I find you need to be fairly generous with the salt and black pepper. Serve.

**This soup freezes well – freeze for up to 3 months. Defrost thoroughly, then reheat gently until piping hot. See page 8 for more guidance on this.**

# Roast Tomato Soup with Basil Dressing

**For this colourful soup, you lightly roast the tomatoes with onions and garlic to concentrate and enhance their flavour – a trick that works wonders with those disappointing tomatoes that look gorgeous but lack a little in the taste department. The basil dressing lifts the whole soup to another dimension and looks so pretty drizzled over the top.**

**Serves 4–6 | Takes 25–30 minutes to make, 10 minutes to cook**

**750g ripe tomatoes, left whole if of the cherry variety, or cut into chunks if larger**
**2 onions, roughly chopped**
**3 cloves garlic, peeled and bruised**
**3 tbsp olive oil**
**salt and freshly ground black pepper**

**For the basil dressing**
**small bunch of fresh basil, leaves roughly torn**
**4 tbsp extra virgin olive oil**
**2 tbsp finely grated fresh Parmesan cheese**
**2 tbsp pine nuts**

Preheat the oven to 180°C/gas 4.

Take a large roasting tin and add the tomatoes, onions and garlic and season with salt and freshly ground black pepper. Pour over the olive oil and toss well to coat. Roast in the oven for 25–30 minutes, stirring once or twice. You are looking for the tomatoes to collapse and soften, but not really to change colour much.

Whilst the tomatoes are in the oven, make the basil dressing by whizzing all the dressing ingredients together in a food processor until smooth. Season to taste with salt and black pepper. If you don't have a food processor, you can make the dressing a little more rustically using a pestle and mortar. Set aside.

Once the tomatoes are ready, you need to purée them, either in a saucepan using a stick blender, or by carefully transferring them to a blender and puréeing until smooth. Add a little cold water to help this process. When you have a smooth, thick purée, you can top up with more water until the soup is the consistency you like – I like mine quite thick but you may prefer yours looser.

Warm the soup gently in a pan until hot, then taste to check the seasoning, adding a little more salt and black pepper, if necessary.

Serve immediately in bowls with the basil dressing drizzled over the top.

**This soup freezes very well so is a great soup to make in batches if you find yourself with a glut of cheap tomatoes during the summer. It will certainly bring a little sunshine into the house when the autumn kicks in. Freeze the soup for up to 3 months. Defrost thoroughly, then reheat gently until piping hot. See page 8 for more guidance on this.**

# Courgette and Stilton Soup

We often get a bit carried away planting courgette seeds. More than anything else I try to grow, they seem to provide maximum crop with the minimum effort... providing the slugs don't get to them first. Whether you grow your own or not, courgettes are really good value during the summer months, and this soup teams them with a strong British cheese to enhance their subtle, dare I say it slightly bland, flavour. Normally a big fan of freshly ground black pepper, for me this soup seems to work best with white pepper, which has a different, more vigorous heat.

**Serves 4–6 | Takes 10 minutes to make, 10 minutes to cook**

**25g unsalted butter**
**1 tbsp olive oil**
**500g courgettes, sliced**
**1–2 cloves garlic, chopped**
**1 tsp dried thyme**
**2 tbsp plain flour**
**500ml milk**
**200–300g Stilton, diced**
**salt and ground white pepper**

Melt the butter with the oil in a large saucepan. Sweat the courgettes, garlic and thyme for 4–5 minutes or until they are slightly softened. Stir in the flour and cook for a further minute.

Pour in the milk and add 250ml cold water, stirring constantly to dissolve the flour, then bring up to a steady simmer. Cook, uncovered, for 5 minutes or so until the courgettes are just tender but still have a little bite.

Carefully transfer the soup to a blender and purée until completely smooth. Return to the pan, add the cubes of Stilton and warm through gently until the cheese just begins to melt. I prefer to leave some lumps of cheese un-melted as I really like discovering the intense little salty bursts in the smooth soup.

Season with a little salt and plenty of white pepper and serve immediately whilst hot, or set aside to cool, then cover and chill for several hours before serving the soup cold.

**This soup freezes well – freeze for up to 3 months. Defrost thoroughly, then reheat gently until piping hot. See page 8 for more guidance on this.**

# Carrot and Coriander Soup

This soup is an absolute classic and it's easy to see why – carrots are cheap, plentiful, sweet and nutritious. By adding the coriander stalks, you get a really intense boost of flavour – it always seems such a waste to throw them out when they have so much to offer. A generous swirl of cream at the end not only looks pretty but adds a delicious softness to this velvety soup.

**Serves 4–6 | Takes 10 minutes to make, 20 minutes to cook**

1 tbsp vegetable oil
700g carrots, sliced
1 large onion, finely chopped
1 clove garlic, crushed
1 litre vegetable stock
small bunch of fresh coriander, leaves and stalks roughly chopped
salt and freshly ground black pepper
single cream and a few fresh coriander leaves, to garnish
crusty granary rolls, to serve (optional)

Heat the oil in a large, heavy-based saucepan and gently sauté the carrots and onion for 5 minutes. Add the garlic and cook for another minute.

Pour over the stock, bring up to a gentle simmer and cook, uncovered, for around 10–15 minutes or until the carrots are just tender.

Add the chopped coriander and cook for a couple more minutes or so until it has just wilted.

Carefully transfer the soup to a blender and purée until really smooth, then return to the pan and reheat gently until hot. If the soup is a little thick, add a splash more water. Season to taste with salt and freshly ground black pepper.

Serve in deep bowls and garnish each portion with a swirl of cream and a few coriander leaves. Serve with crusty granary rolls, if you like, for the perfect accompaniment.

**This soup freezes well – freeze for up to 3 months. Defrost thoroughly, then reheat gently until piping hot. See page 8 for more guidance on this.**

VEGETABLE

# Summer Vegetable Soup with Mint, Coriander and Parsley

This soup is a winner for summer – light, healthy and vibrant and a great way of showcasing the best of the early veg from the garden. Broad beans, peas and green beans are often ripe at the same time and they go so well together. The quality of the stock is very important, so try to make your own if you can or use good quality ready-made stock if not. Pitta crisps are a lovely crunchy accompaniment and any leftover will keep for weeks in an airtight tin – they are great served with dips and a really healthy alternative to deep-fried crisps.

Serves 4–6 | Takes 10 minutes to make, 15 minutes to cook

**1 litre good quality chicken or vegetable stock (homemade is best)**
**150g podded broad beans (about 300g with pods)**
**150g green beans, sliced into 2cm lengths**
**150g podded peas (about 300g with pods)**
**bunch each of fresh mint, fresh coriander and fresh flat-leaf parsley, roughly chopped**
**juice of $\frac{1}{2}$ lemon**
**2 spring onions, finely sliced**

For the pitta crisps
**3 white standard/oval pitta breads**
**extra virgin olive oil**
**salt and freshly ground black pepper**

Preheat the oven to 200°C/gas 6.

First prepare the pitta crisps. Cut the pitta breads into diagonal strips, about 2cm wide. Open up each strip and separate to make 2 pieces, then lay them out in a single layer on a baking sheet. Sprinkle with oil and season with salt and freshly ground black pepper. Bake in the oven for about 15 minutes or until crisp all over. Remove from the oven and transfer to a cooling rack. Set aside.

When the crisps are ready, start the soup by gently heating the stock in a large saucepan. Season well with salt and black pepper. When the stock is simmering, add all the beans and the peas and simmer gently, uncovered, for about 5 minutes or until tender.

Remove the pan from the heat. Stir in the herbs, lemon juice and spring onions and taste to check the seasoning, adding a little more salt and black pepper, if necessary.

Serve the soup in bowls with a few pitta crisps scattered on top of each portion.

**This soup does freeze (without the pitta crisps), but you lose some of the fresh vibrancy of the vegetables once they have been frozen and defrosted. Freeze the soup for up to 3 months. Defrost thoroughly, then reheat gently until piping hot. See page 8 for more guidance on this. Pitta crisps not suitable for freezing, so make these just before serving.**

# Carrot, Lentil and Orange Soup

A wonderful colour, this filling and tasty soup will lift the spirits, whatever the weather. As it all gets puréed up until smooth, this is a good recipe for using up those misshapen carrots you have grown yourself, or those bags of odd-shaped carrots that are so cheap in the supermarket.

**Serves 4–6 | Takes 15 minutes to make, 35 minutes to cook**

2 tbsp olive oil
1 onion, finely chopped
600g carrots, thinly sliced
100g dried red lentils
1 litre vegetable stock
finely grated zest and juice of
   1 large orange
a few fresh sage leaves, finely
   chopped, or 1 tsp dried sage
salt and freshly ground black
   pepper
a little single cream and 3 fresh
   sage leaves, very finely sliced,
   to garnish

Heat the oil in a saucepan and gently fry the onion for 5 minutes or so until it has softened slightly. Stir in the carrots and continue to fry for a further 5 minutes.

Pour in the lentils and stock and bring up to the boil, before adding the orange zest and chopped sage. Reduce the heat and simmer steadily, uncovered, for around 30 minutes or until the carrots are very tender and the lentils are softly collapsing.

Carefully transfer the soup to a blender, in two batches if necessary, and purée until smooth. Return to the pan, add the orange juice and season to taste with salt and freshly ground black pepper. Reheat gently until hot.

I like to serve this soup in deep bowls, garnished with a swirl of cream on top and a little sprinkling of finely sliced sage.

**This soup freezes well (without the garnish) – freeze for up to 3 months. Defrost thoroughly, then reheat gently until piping hot. See page 8 for more guidance on this.**

# Gazpacho

**The perfect dish for a hot summer's day, this chilled Spanish soup is essentially a liquid salad, and it's at its very best when made at the end of the summer when tomatoes are at their ripest and most tasty. As there is no cooking involved, this is the time to use the best quality olive oil you have. This soup really does need to be served very cold, so give yourself plenty of time to chill it in the fridge and serve with a few ice cubes.**

Serves 4–6 | Takes 10 minutes to make, plus soaking the bread, a few hours to chill

100g good quality white bread, crusts removed
1kg very ripe tomatoes, roughly diced
1 red pepper, deseeded and diced
1 green pepper, deseeded and diced
1 cucumber, peeled and diced
2 cloves garlic, crushed
150ml good quality extra virgin olive oil (Spanish, if possible)
2 tbsp sherry vinegar, or to taste
salt and freshly ground black pepper
ice cubes, to serve
roughly chopped fresh flat-leaf parsley and a little good quality extra virgin olive oil, to garnish

Put the bread in a dish, add enough cold water to cover and leave to soak for 15 minutes.

Put the tomatoes, peppers, cucumber, garlic and olive oil in a blender and purée until completely smooth. Squeeze the water out of the bread, add the bread to the soup and blend again, then add enough cold water to thin the soup to the desired consistency.

Pass the soup through a fine sieve into a large bowl. Stir through the sherry vinegar to taste and season with salt and freshly ground black pepper. Cover and chill in the fridge for a good few hours, even overnight wouldn't hurt.

When you are ready to serve, transfer the soup to a serving dish and add a few ice cubes. Garnish with a scattering of parsley and a good drizzle of extra virgin olive oil. Serve with plenty of rustic crusty bread to dip in.

**Not suitable for freezing.**

# Pumpkin, Haricot Bean and Harissa Soup

This filling and hearty soup is a great one for the autumn when pumpkins and squash are cheap and readily available. I would urge you to make your own harissa if you can – the flavour is far more complex than the shop-bought stuff, which I find tends to be all fiery heat rather than the subtle mix of spices it should be.

**Serves 4–6 | Takes 30 minutes to make, plus overnight soaking of the beans, 55 minutes to cook, plus 15 minutes to make the harissa**

**300g dried haricot beans, soaked overnight in cold water, drained and rinsed**
**2 tbsp olive oil**
**1 large onion, chopped**
**600g pumpkin or squash, peeled, deseeded, cut into 2–3cm cubes**
**2 cloves garlic, crushed**
**2 litres vegetable stock**
**2 tbsp sun-dried tomato paste**
**1–2 tbsp harissa (ready-made, or see recipe below)**

**For the harissa**
**1 large red pepper**
**200g medium-hot fresh red chillies, deseeded and roughly chopped**
**4 cloves garlic, chopped**
**6 tbsp extra virgin olive oil**
**3 heaped tsp caraway seeds, coarsely ground**
**3 heaped tsp cumin seeds, coarsely ground**
**1 tbsp tomato purée**
**1 tbsp red wine vinegar**
**2 tbsp Spanish smoked paprika**
**salt and freshly ground black pepper**

Heat the oil in a large saucepan. Fry the onion over medium heat for 5 minutes or until it is beginning to soften and turn translucent. Add the pumpkin, turn up the heat a little and fry for 10–15 minutes or until it is starting to caramelise at the edges. Add the garlic and drained haricot beans, stir briefly, then pour in the stock. Bring up to the boil and boil rapidly for 10 minutes. Turn the heat down to a steady simmer and cook, uncovered, until the beans are soft and tender – this will take around 35–45 minutes, depending on the age of the beans. You may need to add a splash of water if the soup is getting a little thick.

Meanwhile, make the harissa. Blacken the skin of the red pepper – the easiest way to do this is to carefully hold the pepper with a pair of tongs over a gas flame, turning until it is crisp and blackened all over. Alternatively, heat the grill to its highest setting and grill the pepper, turning frequently, until the skin has blackened. Put the pepper in a freezer bag, seal and allow to cool.

Once cool enough to handle, peel off the skin, remove the stalk and deseed the pepper, then roughly chop the flesh. Put the pepper in a food processor, along with the chillies and the rest of the harissa ingredients. Process until really smooth, then season to taste with salt and freshly ground black pepper. Set aside.

Stir the tomato paste and harissa through the hot soup and season to taste with a little salt and black pepper. Serve.

**This soup and the harissa are both suitable for freezing. Freeze them separately – freeze for up to 3 months. Defrost the soup and harissa thoroughly, then reheat the soup gently until piping hot. See page 8 for more guidance on this. Stir the harissa through the reheated soup just before serving.**

# Lettuce, Pea and Mint Soup

**Lettuce, perhaps surprisingly, is very tasty when lightly cooked, and in this soup it is combined with the classic combination of peas and mint. This is a good soup to make on a summers day that is slightly less summery than you would like! As with all subtle-flavoured brothy soups, this one benefits from using a really good-quality stock, so try to make your own if you can (see pages 7–8 for advice on making stock).**

*Serves 4–6 | Takes 10 minutes to make, 10 minutes to cook*

**50g unsalted butter
5 shallots, finely chopped
1 clove garlic, crushed
800ml chicken or vegetable stock
400g podded peas (about 800g
   with pods), fresh or frozen (no
   need to defrost)
2 Little Gem lettuces, separated
   into leaves and torn into
   generous bite-sized pieces
loose handful of fresh mint leaves
salt and freshly ground black
   pepper**

In a heavy-based saucepan, melt the butter over a really low heat, then sweat the shallots and garlic together for around 10 minutes – by this stage, the shallots should be soft and translucent but not at all coloured.

Pour in the stock and bring up to the boil, then lower the heat and simmer, uncovered, for 5 minutes, before adding the peas, lettuce and mint leaves. Cook for a further 5 minutes, by which time the peas should be tender and the lettuce wilted.

Season to taste with salt and freshly ground black pepper and serve. I like to serve this soup simply as it is but you could purée it if you prefer a smooth texture.

**Not suitable for freezing.**

# Bombay Spiced Potato Soup

I first made this soup to jazz up some purple-skinned potatoes I grew. They looked wonderful raw, with their glistening aubergine-coloured skin, but on cooking they were really very floury and disappointingly bland. A few spices and some good quality stock later and they were transformed. I like to add some butter at the end of cooking to enrich this soup a little, but you may or may not be more virtuous than me!

**Serves 4–6 | Takes 15 minutes to make, 20 minutes to cook**

1 tbsp sunflower oil
2 onions, finely chopped
3 cloves garlic, crushed
1 tbsp mustard seeds
1 tbsp ground cumin
1 tbsp black onion seeds (nigella seeds)
$\frac{1}{2}$ tsp ground turmeric
1–2 fresh green chillies, deseeded and chopped
650g potatoes, cut into 1cm cubes
6 tomatoes, finely chopped
1 litre chicken or vegetable stock
small bunch of fresh coriander, roughly chopped
a few knobs of butter (optional)
salt and freshly ground black pepper

Heat the oil in a large saucepan and fry the onions for around 10 minutes or until soft and lightly caramelised. Add the garlic, mustard seeds, cumin, onion seeds, turmeric and chillies and fry for a further minute or two.

Add the potatoes and tomatoes, then pour in the stock. Bring up to the boil, then reduce the heat to a lively simmer and cook, uncovered, for 15–20 minutes or until the potatoes are so tender they are collapsing.

Break the potatoes up a little with the back of a wooden spoon to leave you with a rough and rustic-textured soup. You can use a stick blender in the pan to purée this soup, if you prefer a smoother texture.

Stir through the coriander and butter, if using, and season to taste with salt and freshly ground black pepper. Serve.

**This soup freezes well (without the coriander) – freeze for up to 3 months. Defrost thoroughly, then reheat gently until piping hot. See page 8 for more guidance on this. Stir the chopped coriander through the reheated soup just before serving to liven it up.**

VEGETABLE

# Thai Green Tomato and Coconut Soup

If you have ever grown tomatoes you will know that they never all ripen. Some always stay green and if the summer is a wet one, low on sunshine, then my experience is that they mostly stay green. So this soup began simply as a way of using up my glut – after all there is only so much green tomato chutney you can eat – but I have to say it ended up being so tasty that I shall be seeking out green tomatoes just to make it. It wouldn't really work with red tomatoes as they are just too sweet and not acidic enough. The beauty of sharp green ones is that they balance out the richness of the coconut cream perfectly.

**Serves 4–6 | Takes 25 minutes to make, 15 minutes to cook**

**300g shallots**
**2 medium-hot fresh red or green chillies, deseeded and roughly chopped**
**1 fat lemongrass stalk, roughly chopped**
**3 cloves garlic, chopped**
**3cm piece of fresh root ginger, peeled and grated**
**6 kaffir lime leaves, chopped (fresh or frozen are best, use dried if others are not available)**
**2 tbsp sunflower or vegetable oil**
**800g green tomatoes, roughly chopped**
**600ml vegetable stock**
**500ml coconut cream**
**4 tbsp white basmati rice, rinsed**
**1 tbsp fish sauce (nam pla)**
**1 tbsp jaggery (raw cane sugar) or light soft brown sugar, or to taste**
**juice of $1/2$–1 lime, or to taste**
**salt, to taste**
**small bunch of fresh coriander, roughly chopped**

Put the shallots, chillies, lemongrass, garlic, ginger and lime leaves into a food processor and whizz to a smooth paste.

Heat the oil in a large saucepan and fry the shallot purée for 5–10 minutes or until soft and translucent. Add the green tomatoes and fry for a further 5–10 minutes or until they start to soften and break down.

Pour in the stock and coconut cream, then stir through the rice and fish sauce. Bring up to the boil, then reduce the heat to a steady simmer and cook, uncovered, for about 15 minutes or until the rice and tomatoes are tender.

Turn off the heat and stir through the jaggery, lime juice and salt to taste – you are trying to balance sweet with sour. Finally, stir through the coriander and serve.

**This soup freezes well (without the coriander) – freeze for up to 3 months. Defrost thoroughly, then reheat gently until piping hot. See page 8 for more guidance on this. Stir the chopped coriander through the reheated soup just before serving to liven it up.**

# Creamy Yellow Courgette, Tomato and Anchovy Soup

**Anchovies are not to everyone's taste, but don't be put off – this soup doesn't taste at all fishy, just deeply savoury and interesting. Feel free to use green courgettes if you can't get yellow, they don't really taste any different, I just like the pretty colour of the yellow ones.**

**Serves 4–6 | Takes 15 minutes to make, 5 minutes to cook**

**2 tbsp olive oil**
**500g yellow (or green) courgettes, thinly sliced**
**250g cherry tomatoes, cut in half**
**3 cloves garlic, finely sliced**
**4–6 salted anchovy fillets, rinsed, patted dry and finely chopped**
**3 tbsp fresh oregano or marjoram leaves, roughly chopped**
**800ml hot vegetable stock**
**200ml double cream**
**salt and freshly ground black pepper**
**ciabatta croûtons, to serve (see Cook's Tip)**

Heat the oil in a large pan over a high heat until it is smoking hot. I find a deep, wide frying pan the best for this soup, giving plenty of room for the vegetables to colour nicely. Add the courgettes and tomatoes and fry for around 10 minutes or until softened and caramelised at the edges. Resist the temptation to stir as this will reduce the heat in the pan and prevent the vegetables colouring – simply give the pan an occasional shake from side to side to prevent them catching.

Stir through the garlic, anchovies and oregano and cook for a further minute or two. Pour in the stock, bring up to the boil, then lower the heat and simmer, uncovered, for a few minutes or until the vegetables are tender.

Remove from the heat and stir in the cream. Taste and check the seasoning, adding plenty of freshly ground black pepper and possibly a little salt.

Serve hot in bowls, scattered with the ciabatta croûtons.

**Not suitable for freezing.**

**Cook's Tip**
To make ciabatta croûtons, crumble and tear half a ciabatta loaf into bite-sized pieces and fry in 3–4 tablespoons of olive oil until golden and crisp. Remove from the pan and drain on kitchen paper. Serve scattered over the soup.

# Moroccan Carrot Soup

**The inspiration for this dish was a warm and garlicky carrot salad I ate on a trip to Marrakech. The salad successfully turned the humble carrot squarely to centre stage and this soup, heady with olive oil, garlic, lemon and spices, does the same. This is such a simple 'brothy' soup, I find that really good chicken stock, preferably homemade, creates a richer more unctuous texture. But substitute vegetable stock, if you prefer.**

*Serves 4–6 | Takes 10 minutes to make, 10 minutes to cook*

**1 tbsp cumin seeds**
**1 tbsp coriander seeds**
**6 tbsp olive oil**
**1 tsp paprika**
**$\frac{1}{2}$ tsp ground cinnamon**
**500g carrots, very thinly sliced**
**3 cloves garlic, thinly sliced**
**1–2 fresh red chillies, deseeded
  and finely sliced**
**1 litre good quality chicken stock**
**handful of fresh mint leaves,
  roughly chopped**
**juice of $\frac{1}{2}$ lemon, or to taste**
**salt and freshly ground black
  pepper**

In a large saucepan, dry-fry the cumin and coriander seeds for a minute or two, to toast them. As soon as you smell their aroma wafting up from the pan, tip them into a pestle and mortar and grind coarsely. I urge you not to skip this step – the flavours of cumin and coriander seeds are paramount in this soup and a quick toast in a dry pan will work wonders for their flavour.

Add the oil to the pan and warm gently before returning the crushed spices to the pan, together with the paprika and cinnamon. Add the carrots, garlic and chillies and cook slowly for 5 minutes, gently infusing the slices of carrot with the spices and garlic.

Pour over the stock and bring up to the boil, then lower the heat and simmer, uncovered, for 5 minutes or so until the carrots are soft but not falling apart.

Remove from the heat and stir through the mint. Season to taste with plenty of salt and freshly ground black pepper, then sharpen with a good squeeze of lemon juice. Serve.

**Not suitable for freezing.**

# Summer Minestrone

The beauty of this soup is that there is no set recipe to be followed religiously, I just make it up depending on what I have a glut of, either lurking in the fridge or from the garden. Feel free to experiment with a handful of this and a scattering of that. I would always try to add the onion for the mellow base it gives and keep the quantity of stock the same. A generous drizzle of your best extra virgin olive oil just before serving will really enhance the flavour.

**Serves 4–6 | Takes 10 minutes to make, 15 minutes to cook**

**2 tbsp olive oil**
**1 onion, finely chopped**
**2 cloves garlic, finely chopped**
**6 generous handfuls of prepared mixed vegetables, cut into bite-sized pieces (such as carrots, tomatoes, courgettes, podded peas or broad beans, French or runner beans)**
**75g long grain white rice**
**1 litre chicken or vegetable stock**
**small bunch of fresh basil, leaves roughly torn**
**salt and freshly ground black pepper**
**extra virgin olive oil, to serve**

Heat the olive oil in a large saucepan and gently sweat the onion for 10 minutes or until soft and translucent. Add the garlic and fry for a further minute.

Stir through the vegetables and rice, then pour in the stock and season with a little salt and freshly ground black pepper. Bring up to the boil, then lower the heat and simmer, uncovered, for around 15 minutes or until the vegetables and rice are cooked and tender.

Taste to check the seasoning, adding a little more salt and black pepper, if necessary, then stir through the basil. Serve the soup in bowls, drizzled with plenty of extra virgin olive oil.

**This soup does freeze, but depending on the selection of vegetables you use, a little bit of texture may be lost on defrosting – freeze for up to 3 months. Defrost thoroughly, then reheat gently until piping hot. See page 8 for more guidance on this.**

# Jerusalem Artichoke, Butter Bean and Parsley Soup

**I don't grow Jerusalem artichokes in my garden but they seem to be ubiquitous to the veg box schemes that are so popular these days. I do however grow flat-leaf parsley, I can't get enough of the stuff, and I would even stick my neck on the line and say it's among my very favourite cooking ingredients. This soup uses a big fat bunch, adding not only a fragrant sweet flavour but turning it a gorgeous green colour.**

**Serves 4–6 | Takes 15 minutes to make, 20 minutes to cook**

**2 tbsp olive oil
1 onion, chopped
600g Jerusalem artichokes, scrubbed and cut into 1cm slices
400g can butter beans, drained and rinsed
1 litre vegetable stock
generous bunch of fresh flat-leaf parsley, leaves and stalks roughly chopped
salt and freshly ground black pepper
a little single cream and a few fresh parsley leaves, to garnish**

Heat the oil in a large saucepan and sweat the onion gently for 5 minutes, by which time it should be softening slightly. Add the artichoke slices and drained butter beans, then pour over the stock.

Bring up to the boil, then reduce the heat and simmer for around 15 minutes or until the artichokes are very nearly soft. Add the chopped parsley and cook for a further 5 minutes.

Carefully transfer the soup to a blender, in two batches if necessary, and purée until really smooth. Pass the soup through a sieve back into a clean pan, then reheat gently until hot.

Taste to check the seasoning, adding a little salt and plenty of freshly ground black pepper. Serve the soup in bowls and garnish each portion with a swirl of cream and a few parsley leaves.

**This soup freezes well – freeze for up to 3 months. Defrost thoroughly, then reheat gently until piping hot. See page 8 for more guidance on this.**

# Yellow Pepper and Chorizo Soup with Goat's Cheese

**Best made mid-summer when sweet yellow peppers are cheap and plentiful, this tasty soup is really colourful and slightly spicy.**

Serves 4–6 |Takes 15 minutes to make, 15 minutes to cook

1 tbsp olive oil
100g piece of chorizo, thinly sliced
4 large yellow peppers, deseeded
   and sliced
2–3 cloves garlic, sliced
1 litre chicken or vegetable stock
small bunch of fresh flat-leaf
   parsley, chopped
salt and freshly ground black
   pepper
125g soft goat's cheese, crumbled,
   to serve

Heat the oil in a large saucepan until it is smoking hot. Toss in the chorizo and fry for a few minutes until crisp. Remove half of the chorizo to a plate and set aside for the garnish – I find it best to cover the plate with foil, purely to stop me picking!

Add the sliced peppers to the remaining chorizo in the pan and fry over a high heat for around 10 minutes, stirring from time to time, until the peppers are starting to soften and colour a little at the edges.

Stir through the garlic and fry for a further minute, before carefully pouring over the stock – it may hiss and spit a little as the pan will be really hot. Reduce the heat and let the soup simmer, uncovered, for around 10 minutes or until the peppers are cooked through.

Purée the soup to the desired consistency, either using a stick blender in the pan, or carefully transfer the soup to a blender and purée until smooth, then return to the pan and reheat gently until hot. Stir through the parsley and season to taste with salt and freshly ground black pepper.

Serve the soup in bowls, scattered with the reserved chorizo and the crumbled goat's cheese.

**This soup freezes well (without the goat's cheese), although peppers can loose a little texture and become soggy on defrosting, so if you plan to freeze it, purée the soup until smooth before freezing. Freeze the soup for up to 3 months. Defrost thoroughly, then reheat gently until piping hot. See page 8 for more guidance on this.**

# Roast Aubergine and Borlotti Bean Soup with Mozzarella

I originally made this soup using the vivid red and white borlotti beans that had been growing in a tangle at the end of my garden. But as it's not easy to get hold of these beans fresh unless you grow them yourself, I've given the recipe to use canned beans. Feel free to substitute the equivalent weight of fresh or cooked dried beans. Once the soup is served in bowls, I sprinkle over little cubes of mozzarella to stir through and melt as you eat. Delicious.

**Serves 4–6 | Takes 30–35 minutes to make, 10 minutes to cook**

2 fat aubergines, cut into 1cm dice
1 large red onion, finely chopped
4 tbsp olive oil
3 sprigs of fresh rosemary
250g cherry tomatoes, quartered
3 cloves garlic, crushed
1 litre vegetable stock
400g can borlotti beans, rinsed
   and drained
salt and freshly ground black
   pepper
small bunch of fresh basil, leaves
   roughly torn, to garnish
2 balls of mozzarella, cut into 1cm
   cubes, to serve

Preheat the oven to 160°C/gas 3.

In a large roasting tin, toss the aubergines and red onion in the oil. Tuck in the rosemary sprigs and season well with salt and freshly ground black pepper. Roast in the oven for 15 minutes, then remove the tin from the oven and stir through the cherry tomatoes and garlic. Return to the oven and roast for a further 15–20 minutes or so until the vegetables are tender.

Scrape the roasted vegetables, along with all the juices, into a large saucepan. Rinse out the roasting tin with a little of the stock to release any lovely caramelised bits off the bottom, then pour any scrapings and the remaining stock into the pan and add the drained borlotti beans. Bring up to the boil, then lower the heat and simmer, uncovered, for about 5 minutes to ensure the beans are heated through.

Taste to check the seasoning, adding a little more salt and black pepper, if necessary. Serve the hot soup in bowls, garnish with the basil and then scatter some mozzarella cubes over each portion.

**This soup can be frozen (without the basil and mozzarella) but the aubergine loses a little bit of texture on defrosting, so this soup is best served fresh. If you do freeze the soup, freeze it (without the basil and mozzarella) for up to 3 months. Defrost thoroughly, then reheat gently until piping hot. See page 8 for more guidance on this. Garnish the reheated soup with basil and scatter over the mozzarella cubes just before serving.**

# Smoky Roast Beetroot Soup with Bacon and Garlicky Crème Fraîche

**When I grow beetroot they emerge from the soil in all shapes and sizes, making it impossible to cook them evenly if left whole. So, I usually chop them up and roast them, which really concentrates their earthy flavour.**

**Serves 4–6 | Takes 45 minutes to make, 10 minutes to cook**

**800g raw beetroot, peeled and cut into 1cm chunks**
**2 tbsp olive oil**
**1 tsp Spanish smoked paprika**
**2 sprigs of fresh thyme or 1 tsp dried thyme**
**12 rashers smoked streaky bacon**
**1 litre vegetable or chicken stock**
**salt and freshly ground black pepper**

**For the garlicky crème fraîche**
**4 tbsp crème fraîche**
**1–2 cloves garlic, crushed**
**a sprig of fresh thyme, leaves picked and finely chopped**

Preheat the oven to 180°C/gas 4.

Tip the beetroot chunks into a roasting tin and toss them with the oil, smoked paprika and thyme sprigs. Season with salt and freshly ground black pepper. Cover the tin loosely with foil and roast in the oven for 25 minutes. The foil allows the beetroot to steam as it roasts, so speeding up the cooking process.

Whilst the beetroot is cooking, prepare the garlicky crème fraîche by mixing all the ingredients together in a small bowl. Season to taste with salt and black pepper and set aside.

Remove the roasting tin from the oven, discard the foil and lay the rashers of bacon over the top of the beetroot. Return to the oven and roast, uncovered, for about 20 minutes or until the bacon is crisp and the beetroot is tender.

Remove from the oven, then remove the bacon to a plate and keep warm. Snip the bacon into pieces just before serving.

Pour the stock into the roasting tin and scrape and stir to release any nice caramelised bits off the bottom, then carefully transfer the whole lot to a saucepan.

Purée the soup to the desired consistency using a stick blender in the pan, then bring back up to a gentle simmer. Taste to check the seasoning, adding a little more salt and black pepper, if necessary.

Serve the soup in bowls, topped with the garlicky crème fraîche and the crisp bacon pieces.

**This soup does freeze (without the garlicky crème fraîche and bacon garnishes) but the lumps of beetroot tend to be a bit watery on defrosting, so if you plan to freeze it, purée the soup until smooth before freezing. The soup will freeze for up to 3 months. Defrost thoroughly, then reheat gently until piping hot. See page 8 for more guidance on this. Garlicky crème fraîche and bacon garnishes not suitable for freezing, so make or cook these just before serving.**

# Chilled Cucumber, Avocado and Yogurt Soup

**This is a cool soup for a hot summer's day with all the fresh flavours of that lovely Greek dip, tzatziki. The avocado, whilst not traditional in tzatziki, adds a smooth, creamy texture that works very nicely. It is good served with crispy toasted pitta bread, and perhaps a few Kalamata olives scattered on top.**

*Serves 4–6 | Takes 10 minutes to make, several hours to chill*

**2 cucumbers, cut into 1cm cubes**
**1 avocado, cut in half, stone removed and flesh scooped out**
**2 cloves garlic, crushed**
**500ml natural yogurt (preferably Greek-style yogurt)**
**small handful of fresh mint leaves, finely chopped**
**salt and freshly ground black pepper**
**good quality extra virgin olive oil, a few Kalamata olives and toasted pitta bread, to serve**

Put most of the cucumber into a blender (reserving a little for the garnish), together with the avocado flesh, garlic and yogurt. Purée the mixture until it is completely smooth, adding enough cold water to give the consistency of double cream.

Pass the soup through a sieve into a large bowl and stir through the mint. Season to taste with salt and freshly ground black pepper.

Cover and chill in the fridge for at least 2–3 hours or until the soup is really cold. You can speed up the chilling process by placing the bowl in the freezer for about an hour or so, stirring from time to time to prevent ice crystals forming.

When the soup is really cold, serve it in chilled bowls. Drizzle each portion with a little really good quality extra virgin olive oil, then scatter over the reserved cucumber, along with the olives. Serve with toasted pitta bread.

**Not suitable for freezing.**

# Squash Soup with Toasted Pine Nuts, Raisins and Cinnamon

**One of the vegetables I seem to have most success growing in my garden is squash. This year I grew Marina di Chioggia, a luminous yellow-fleshed Venetian variety. Whilst my plants only yielded 8 or so fruits, each individual squash was enormous, giving enough flesh for several meals. Once I cut into the squash, I wrapped any leftover tightly in cling film and stored it in the fridge where it lasted for over 10 days. Consequently, there has been much squash recipe experimenting in our house, and this vaguely Middle Eastern soup was one of the success stories.**

**Serves 4–6 | Takes 15 minutes to make, 25 minutes to cook**

**1 onion, chopped**
**2 tbsp olive oil**
**2 cloves garlic, crushed**
**1 tsp ground cumin**
**1 tsp ground cinnamon**
**a pinch of dried red chilli flakes, or to taste**
**1kg squash or pumpkin, peeled, deseeded and cut into 2–3cm chunks**
**1 litre vegetable stock**
**salt and freshly ground black pepper**
**small handful of fresh coriander leaves, roughly chopped, to serve**

**For the garnish**
**2 tbsp olive oil**
**4 tbsp pine nuts**
**4 tbsp raisins**
**1 tsp ground cinnamon**

In a large saucepan, fry the onion in the oil for about 10 minutes or until soft and golden. Add the garlic, cumin, cinnamon and chilli flakes and fry for a further minute.

Stir through the chunks of squash and pour in the stock. Bring up to the boil, then lower the heat and simmer, uncovered, for around 20 minutes or until the squash is soft and collapsing.

Carefully transfer the soup to a blender and purée until smooth, then return to the pan and season to taste with salt and freshly ground black pepper. Reheat gently until hot.

Whilst the soup is simmering, make the garnish. Heat the oil in a small frying pan and add the pine nuts, raisins and cinnamon. Fry over a medium heat for 2–3 minutes, stirring constantly to make sure the mixture doesn't burn. When the pine nuts are toasted and golden brown, tip them into a small bowl, scraping out all the sticky bits of raisins and cinnamon. Set aside.

Serve the hot soup in bowls. Scatter each portion with a tablespoon or so of the garnish and sprinkle with a little chopped coriander.

**This soup freezes well (without the garnish) – freeze for up to 3 months. Defrost thoroughly, then reheat gently until piping hot. See page 8 for more guidance on this. Garnish not suitable for freezing, so make this just before serving.**

# LUXURIOUS

Contrary to popular belief, soup can be an extravagance. The addition of glorious seasonal seafood, rich cream and alcohol, or exquisite vegetables, can turn something humble into something really rather luxurious. Serve these soups when you want to impress your guests or when you simply feel like spoiling your loved ones with something truly special.

# Smoked Salmon Soup with Cream and Dill

When I was a child, smoked salmon used to be a real (and very rare) treat reserved for holidays and high days. Now it's much more readily and cheaply available. But to me it still tastes rich and luxurious, and in this soup it is combined with plenty of wine and cream, definitely not frugal ingredients.

**Serves 4–6 | Takes 10 minutes to make, 15 minutes to cook**

50g unsalted butter
1 large onion, finely chopped
400g potatoes, finely diced
1 clove garlic, crushed
200ml white wine
700ml light chicken stock
400g smoked salmon, cut into
  bite-sized pieces
200ml double cream
2 tbsp finely chopped fresh dill
salt and freshly ground black
  pepper
a few fresh dill sprigs, a few extra
  pieces of smoked salmon and a
  little extra double cream, to
  garnish

Melt the butter in a large saucepan and gently fry the onion for 5 minutes or until slightly softened. Add the potatoes and garlic and fry for a couple more minutes, before adding the wine and stock. Bring up to the boil, then lower the heat and simmer, uncovered, until the potato is soft – this will take around 10–15 minutes depending on the size of your potato pieces.

Stir through half of the smoked salmon. Carefully transfer the soup to a blender and purée until completely smooth, then return to the pan. Pour in the cream, add the chopped dill and the remaining smoked salmon and season to taste with a little salt and freshly ground black pepper. Heat gently for a few minutes until hot, taking care not to break up the salmon pieces too much as you stir.

Serve the soup in bowls and garnish each portion with a sprig of dill, a few pieces of smoked salmon and a little more double cream.

**This soup freezes well (without the garnishes) – freeze for up to 3 months. Defrost thoroughly, then reheat gently until piping hot. See page 8 for more guidance on this. Garnishes not suitable for freezing, so simply add these just before serving.**

# Field Mushroom Soup with Sherry and Pan-Fried Sea Bream

**This earthy soup is rich with sherry and cream, and the fish fillets floating on top turn it into a really special lunch or light supper dish. In season, you could use a few fresh wild mushrooms in place of some of the field mushrooms, if you like.**

**Serves 4–6 | Takes 10 minutes to make, 15 minutes to cook**

**2 tbsp olive oil**
**50g unsalted butter**
**1kg field mushrooms, sliced**
**1 onion, chopped**
**1 clove garlic, chopped**
**3 sprigs of fresh thyme**
**75ml rich dry sherry (such as dry Oloroso)**
**1.2 litres vegetable stock**
**150ml double cream**
**2–3 black sea bream fillets with skin-on (about 180g each, allowing $\frac{1}{2}$ a fillet per portion), cut in half widthways**
**salt and freshly ground black pepper**
**finely chopped fresh flat-leaf parsley, to garnish**

Heat the oil and half of the butter in a large saucepan and add the mushrooms, onion, garlic, thyme and a good grinding of black pepper. Sauté gently for around 10 minutes or until the mushrooms have wilted and are just beginning to caramelise.

Add the sherry and fry for a few minutes or until it has been absorbed by the mushrooms. Pour in the stock and bring up to the boil, then turn down the heat and simmer, uncovered, for 10 minutes. Remove and discard the thyme sprigs.

Carefully transfer the soup to a blender and purée until really smooth, then return to the pan. Pour in the cream, stir thoroughly and bring up to a gentle simmer. Taste to check the seasoning, adding a little more salt and black pepper, if necessary. Keep warm whilst you cook the fish.

Season the fish fillets on both sides with salt and black pepper. Melt the remaining butter in a frying pan over a medium heat. When it starts to foam, add the fish fillets, skin-side down. Cook for 3–4 minutes or until the skin is crisp and golden, then turn over and cook for a further minute.

Serve the hot soup in bowls with a piece of fish on top of each portion and garnish with a sprinkle of chopped parsley.

**This soup freezes well (without the fish) – freeze for up to 3 months. Defrost thoroughly, then reheat gently until piping hot. See page 8 for more guidance on this. Fried fish fillets not suitable for freezing, so simply cook these as directed and add to the reheated soup just before serving.**

# Cream of Asparagus Soup

When in season asparagus is not a particularly expensive vegetable, but this rich, creamy soup still tastes pretty posh to me! Before you add the cream, taste the soup – if the asparagus is a little 'stringy' as it can sometimes be, especially towards the end of season, it is best to sieve the soup before serving to get a super smooth texture.

**Serves 4–6 | Takes 10 minutes to make, 15 minutes to cook**

**50g unsalted butter**
**1 large onion, finely chopped**
**2 bunches (about 500g) of asparagus (woody ends trimmed off), cut into 2cm pieces, tips reserved separately**
**1 tbsp plain flour**
**1 litre chicken or vegetable stock**
**150ml double cream**
**salt and freshly ground black pepper**

Melt the butter in a large saucepan and gently sweat the onion for 5 minutes or until it is beginning to turn translucent. Add the asparagus (reserving the tips separately) and sweat for a further 10 minutes.

Sprinkle over the flour and stir thoroughly to break up any lumps. Pour over the stock and bring up to a gentle simmer, stirring. Cook, uncovered, until the asparagus is tender – about 10–15 minutes.

Carefully transfer the soup to a blender and purée until completely smooth, then return to the pan. Do this in batches, if necessary. If the soup remains a little stringy after blending, pass it through a sieve as you return it to the pan. Bring back to a gentle simmer and then stir through the cream. Season to taste with a little salt and plenty of freshly ground black pepper.

Meanwhile, steam or boil the reserved asparagus tips over or in a separate pan of boiling water for about 5 minutes or until just tender. Serve the soup in bowls, garnished with the asparagus tips.

**This soup freezes well – freeze for up to 3 months. Defrost thoroughly, then reheat gently until piping hot. See page 8 for more guidance on this.**

# Smoked Fish Chowder

**Creamy, smoky, rich and filling, this soup ticks lots of satisfying boxes for me. Sometimes I like to embellish it with a poached egg to turn it into an even more hearty meal – perfect comfort food for chilly nights.**

**Serves 4–6 | Takes 20 minutes to make, 25 minutes to cook**

**500g un-dyed smoked haddock fillets (with skin on)**
**300ml milk**
**2 bay leaves**
**$\frac{1}{2}$ tsp black peppercorns, crushed in a pestle and mortar**
**50g unsalted butter**
**2 leeks, washed and finely sliced**
**2 sticks celery, finely chopped**
**2 carrots, finely chopped**
**2 potatoes, cut into 1cm dice**
**2 cloves garlic, crushed**
**2 tsp plain flour**
**600ml vegetable stock**
**200ml white wine**
**200g smoked salmon, cut into strips**
**200g cooked, peeled prawns**
**125ml double cream**
**salt and freshly ground black pepper**
**small bunch of fresh flat-leaf parsley, roughly chopped, and lemon wedges, to serve**

Poach the fish by laying the fillets in a single layer in a deep frying pan, cutting them to fit, if necessary. Pour over the milk, tuck in the bay leaves and sprinkle with the crushed peppercorns. Dot the surface with half of the butter and bring up to the boil. Reduce the heat to a simmer and cover tightly with a lid or a piece of foil. Cook for 5–8 minutes or until the fish is opaque and flakes easily. Remove the pan from the heat. Using a fish slice, transfer the fish to a plate and reserve the poaching milk.

Melt the remaining butter in a large saucepan and gently sweat the leeks, celery, carrots, potatoes and garlic together for around 10 minutes or until the vegetables are beginning to soften. Stir through the flour.

Pour in the reserved poaching milk, discarding the bay leaves, along with the stock and wine. Stir well to ensure that there are no lumpy bits of flour left, then bring up to a steady simmer, stirring, and cook, uncovered, for around 15–20 minutes or until the vegetables are soft and tender.

Flake in the smoked haddock, discarding the skin and taking care to remove any tiny bones that may be hiding, then add the smoked salmon and prawns. Gently warm through whilst stirring in the cream, then season to taste with a little salt and plenty more freshly ground black pepper.

Serve the soup in bowls, scattered with a little chopped parsley and with lemon wedges to squeeze over.

**Not suitable for freezing.**

SEAFOOD

# Crab, Cream and Brandy Soup

I adore the flavour of crab which to my mind tastes far superior to the more expensive lobster, and is much more sustainable to fish. This really easy soup uses an equal mix of white meat for texture, and brown meat for flavour. It's lovely served with generously buttered hunks of bread cut from a crusty granary loaf.

**Serves 4–6 | Takes 15 minutes to make, 20 minutes to cook**

50g unsalted butter
1 large onion, finely chopped
1 stick celery, finely chopped
1 carrot, finely chopped
1 clove garlic, crushed
1 tbsp plain flour
800ml fish stock (preferably
   homemade – see page 56)
1 tbsp tomato purée
150ml double cream
400g fresh crab meat (half white
   meat and half brown meat)
60–80ml brandy, or to taste
salt and freshly ground black
   pepper
a little extra double cream and a
   few snipped fresh chives, to
   garnish

Gently melt the butter in a large saucepan and sweat the onion, celery and carrot together for 10 minutes or until softened but not coloured. Add the garlic and cook for a further minute, before stirring through the flour, mixing well to break up any lumps.

Pour in the stock and bring up to the boil, stirring, then reduce the heat. Stir through the tomato purée and season with a little salt and freshly ground black pepper. Simmer gently, uncovered, for 15 minutes. Add the cream, crab meat and brandy and simmer for a further 5 minutes.

Taste to check the seasoning, adding a little more salt and black pepper, if necessary. Serve the soup in bowls, garnished with a little drizzle of cream and a few chives.

**This soup is best made fresh, so is not suitable for freezing.**

# Celeriac Soup with Serrano Ham and Red Onion, Sage and Black Olive Salsa

Celeriac, with its distinctive celery-like taste and creamy texture, makes a lovely, smooth-textured soup that is really economical to serve to a crowd. However, this version is embellished with a punchy salsa of red onions and black olives and garnished with strips of sweet Serrano ham, making it fancy enough to serve for a special occasion.

**Serves 4–6 | Takes 20 minutes to make, 20 minutes to cook**

**For the soup**
juice of $^1/_2$ lemon
1 large celeriac
2 tbsp olive oil
1 onion, chopped
2 floury potatoes (such as Desiree, King Edward or Maris Piper)
1 clove garlic, crushed
1 litre vegetable stock
150ml double cream
salt and freshly ground black pepper

**For the salsa**
1 red onion, very finely chopped
handful of pitted black olives, finely chopped
4 fresh sage leaves, very finely chopped
2 tbsp best quality extra virgin olive oil
1 tbsp sherry vinegar

4 slices of Serrano ham, torn into strips, to garnish

Make the soup. Celeriac quickly oxidizes and turns brown once you have peeled it, so before you make the first cut, have ready a large bowl of cold water into which you have squeezed the lemon juice. Peel and chop the celeriac into 2cm pieces, plunging the pieces into the acidulated water as you go.

Heat the olive oil in a large saucepan and sweat the onion for 10 minutes or so until soft and translucent. Drain the celeriac and add it to the pan, along with the potatoes and garlic, and fry for a further 10 minutes.

Pour in the stock, bring up to a steady simmer and cook, uncovered, until the vegetables are soft – this will take about 15–20 minutes.

Carefully transfer the soup to a blender and purée until really smooth, then return to the pan. Stir in the cream, warm through gently and then season to taste with salt and freshly ground black pepper.

To make the salsa, combine the red onion, black olives and sage in a small bowl. Add the extra virgin olive oil and sherry vinegar, tasting as you go to get a good balance between sweet and sharp.

Serve the hot soup in bowls with a spoonful of salsa on top of each portion, and garnish each bowlful with a few strips of the Serrano ham.

**This soup freezes well (without salsa and ham garnish) – freeze for up to 3 months. Defrost thoroughly, then reheat gently until piping hot. See page 8 for more guidance on this. Salsa and ham garnish not suitable for freezing, so simply make the salsa and add the ham garnish just before serving.**

# Bouillabaisse

**This wonderfully rich fish soup hails from Provence in southern France and for me it is the essence of the Med in a bowl. Served with plenty of baguette slices and rouille – a punchy red pepper and garlic sauce – this soup is great for entertaining friends. My idea of the perfect dinner party is serving a big generous bowl of something delicious that your guests can help themselves to, and this fits the bill perfectly.**

Serves 4–6 | Takes 1 hour to make, 30 minutes to cook

**For the fish stock**
bones from the fish (see below)
heads from the prawns (see below)
2 sticks celery, sliced
2 carrots, sliced
1 large onion, sliced
handful of fresh parsley, stalks and leaves
2 bay leaves
6 black peppercorns
1 tsp fennel seeds

**For the soup**
500g fresh mussels (in shell)
4 tbsp olive oil
2 leeks, washed and finely sliced
2 fennel bulbs, trimmed and finely sliced
3 cloves garlic, crushed
10–12 new potatoes (standard size not baby ones), sliced
6 plum tomatoes, skinned and chopped
2–3 wide strips of pared orange peel
2 bay leaves
a pinch of saffron threads
2–3 tbsp Pernod
2kg mixed white fish (such as sea bass, bream, gurnard, monkfish), filleted (bones reserved for stock)
12 large, raw shell-on king prawns, heads cut off and reserved for stock

**For the rouille**
1 red pepper
2 cloves garlic, crushed
1 tsp cayenne pepper
125ml best quality extra virgin olive oil
3 tbsp fresh white breadcrumbs
a squeeze of lemon juice, or to taste
salt and freshly ground black pepper

handful of chopped fresh flat-leaf parsley, to garnish
1 baguette, cut into slices, to serve

Make the fish stock first by putting all the stock ingredients into a large saucepan. Add 2 litres cold water and bring slowly up to the boil. Turn the heat down and simmer gently, uncovered, for 30 minutes, skimming off and discarding any scum that rises to the surface.

Remove from the heat and strain the liquid into a clean saucepan. Discard the contents of the strainer. Bring the liquid up to the boil, then boil rapidly until reduced by about half – you are looking for a generous litre (1–1.2 litres) of concentrated stock. Don't be tempted to reduce the stock with the bones still in, they will spoil the flavour and turn the stock cloudy.

Whilst the stock is simmering, prepare the mussels for the soup by washing them thoroughly under cold running water. Pull off any beards and discard any mussels that do not shut firmly when tapped against the edge of the sink. Place the mussels in a bowl and set aside in the fridge.

SEAFOOD

You can also make the rouille now. Preheat the grill to high. Grill the red pepper until the skin is blackened all over, then remove it from the heat. Leave the pepper to cool a little, then peel and deseed it. Put the red pepper flesh into a blender, along with the garlic and cayenne pepper. Blend to a paste, then, with the motor running, slowly add the extra virgin olive oil. Finally, add the breadcrumbs to bind the sauce, and sharpen to taste with a squeeze of lemon juice, then season with salt and freshly ground black pepper.

Transfer the rouille to a serving bowl and set aside at room temperature to allow the flavours to develop.

When the stock has reduced, make the soup. Heat the olive oil in a large, heavy-based saucepan and gently sweat the leeks, fennel and garlic for a few minutes or until they begin to soften and turn translucent, being careful not to let them colour. Add the potatoes, tomatoes, orange peel and bay leaves and cook for a further couple of minutes.

Add the saffron threads, then pour over the reduced stock and the Pernod and bring up to a steady simmer. Season with salt and black pepper and cover the pan with a tight-fitting lid. Cook for around 15–20 minutes or until the potatoes are soft but not disintegrating.

Whilst the soup is simmering, cut the fish fillets into even-sized pieces, each about 5–6cm. When the potatoes are done, float the fish pieces on top of the soup, re-cover and cook for a further 4–5 minutes.

Add the prepared mussels and prawns, turning them gently in the stock but trying not to break up the fish too much. Re-cover and cook for a further 4–5 minutes, by which time the fish and prawns will be cooked and the mussels will have opened. Discard any unopened mussels, then remove and discard the orange peel and bay leaves. Taste to check the seasoning, adding a little more salt and black pepper, if necessary.

Serve the soup in deep bowls with the chopped parsley scattered over the top to garnish. Serve the bowl of rouille and the baguette slices on the side.

**Not suitable for freezing.**

# Roast Garlic and Bean Soup with Sage Butter

This is a frugal soup in disguise – the sage butter drizzled over at the end adds a touch of nutty luxury to balance out the simplicity of the beans. Don't be alarmed by the quantity of garlic in this recipe – long, slow roasting really mellows and softens the flavour, rendering it intensely sweet and nutty.

**Serves 4–6 | Takes 10 minutes to make, plus overnight soaking of the beans, up to $1\frac{1}{2}$ hours to cook**

**For the soup**
**500g dried cannellini beans, soaked overnight in cold water, drained and rinsed**
**4 fat heads garlic, left whole**
**3 sprigs each of fresh rosemary and fresh thyme**
**3 bay leaves**
**1 litre vegetable stock**
**salt and freshly ground black pepper**

**For the caramelised sage butter**
**75g unsalted butter**
**12 fresh sage leaves, sliced into thin strips**

Preheat the oven to 160°C/gas 3.

Make the soup. Place the garlic on a baking tray and roast in the oven for around 30–40 minutes or until soft. Remove from the oven and leave to cool.

Whilst the garlic is roasting, cook the cannellini beans. Add the drained beans to a large saucepan and cover with cold water to a level of about 2cm above the beans. Tie the herb sprigs and bay leaves into a little bundle with a piece of string and add to the beans. Bring up to the boil and boil rapidly for 10 minutes, then reduce the heat to a steady simmer and cook, uncovered, for around $1–1\frac{1}{2}$ hours or until the beans are soft and tender. The time it takes for the beans to soften will vary hugely depending on their age. Keep half an eye on the beans, adding a splash more cold water every now and then if they are drying out – you are aiming to be left with the soft beans in a little water rather than swimming in water.

Fish out and discard the herbs, then pour in the stock and bring up to the boil. Gently squeeze the roasted garlic flesh out of its skin on to a plate, squidge to a purée with the back of a knife and then add it to the pan, stirring well to mix the garlic evenly through the soup.

Carefully pour half of the soup into a blender and whizz until smooth, then return to the rest of the soup in the pan and reheat gently. Season to taste with salt and freshly ground black pepper. Keep warm whilst you prepare the sage butter.

For the caramelised sage butter, melt the butter in a small, heavy-based saucepan over a medium heat. When it starts to foam, add the sage and fry until the leaves turn crisp and the butter has caramelised to a golden, nutty brown colour. Keep an eagle eye on it – you are treading a fine line between caramelised and burnt. As soon as the butter is ready, pour it into a warmed bowl to stop it cooking further.

Serve the soup in bowls with the caramelised sage butter drizzled over the top.

**This soup freezes well (without the caramelised sage butter) – freeze for up to 3 months. Defrost thoroughly, then reheat gently until piping hot. See page 8 for more guidance on this. Caramelised sage butter not suitable for freezing, so simply make this just before serving.**

# Cream of Watercress Soup with Brie Toasts

Watercress is a wonderful thing – its peppery leaves are great for perking up a salad or sandwich. But it is equally good lightly cooked, such as in this easy soup which, served with oozing brie on toast, makes a very lovely lunch. I use granary bread as I love the contrast in textures between the nubbly bits of bread and the silky smooth melted cheese, but use white or wholemeal bread, if you prefer.

**Serves 4–6 | Takes 20 minutes to make, 15–20 minutes to cook**

**For the soup**
**50g unsalted butter**
**5 shallots, finely chopped**
**1 clove garlic, crushed**
**2 potatoes, cut into 1cm cubes**
**3 bunches of watercress (about 300g), washed**
**1.2 litres vegetable stock**
**100ml single cream**
**salt and freshly ground black pepper**

**For the brie toasts**
**4 thick slices of bread**
**250g firm brie, cut into slices**

For the soup, melt the butter in a large saucepan over a low heat, then add the shallots and sweat gently for 10 minutes or until they are soft and translucent but not coloured at all. Add the garlic and potatoes and continue to fry gently for a further 10 minutes.

Pick over the watercress, discarding only the tough, thicker stems, and roughly chop it. Add to the pan, stirring well to mix, then pour over the stock and season with a little salt and freshly ground black pepper. Bring up to the boil, then lower the heat and simmer, uncovered, for 10–15 minutes or until the potatoes are tender and the watercress has wilted down.

Carefully transfer the soup to a blender and purée until really smooth, then return to the pan. Taste to check the seasoning, adding a little more salt and black pepper, if necessary, then stir through the cream. Reheat gently, taking care not to let the soup boil or the cream may separate.

To make the brie toasts, preheat the grill to medium. Toast the bread slices under the grill on one side. Remove from the grill, turn the bread slices over and lay the brie slices over the untoasted sides. Return to the grill for a few minutes until the cheese has started to melt and bubble. Remove from the grill and season the toasts with a little black pepper, then cut each slice into wedges.

Serve the hot soup in bowls with the brie toasts on the side.

**This soup freezes well (without brie toasts and preferably without the cream) – freeze for up to 3 months. Defrost thoroughly, then reheat gently until piping hot. See page 8 for more guidance on this. If you have not frozen leftovers, stir the cream into the reheated soup. Brie toasts not suitable for freezing, so simply make these just before serving.**

FISH

# Fresh Pea Soup with Smoked Trout and Horseradish Cream

**It always feels such a dreadful waste to throw away the pea pods after podding fresh peas. In this soup they are used to make a simple but sweet stock. I like to garnish this with a few pea shoots, snipped from the garden in early summer. Supermarkets seem to have caught on how sweet and delicious pea shoots are and they can often now be found alongside the salads.**

**Serves 4–6 | Takes 35 minutes to make, 10 minutes to cook**

**For the soup**
**1kg fresh peas (weight with pods)**
**50g unsalted butter**
**200g shallots, finely chopped**
**salt and freshly ground black pepper**
**2–3 skinless smoked trout fillets (about 150g total weight, allowing $1/2$ a fillet per portion), to serve**
**a few fresh pea shoots, to garnish**

**For the horseradish cream**
**4 tbsp crème fraîche**
**about 1 tbsp peeled and grated fresh horseradish, or to taste (or if unavailable, use horseradish sauce instead)**

Make the soup. Pod the peas, setting the peas aside in a bowl and throwing the pods into a large saucepan. Cover the pods with 1.5 litres cold water. Bring up to the boil, then reduce the heat to a steady simmer and cook, uncovered, for 20 minutes. Use a slotted spoon to scoop out the pods and discard them. Continue to simmer the stock for another 15 minutes or so until it has reduced by about one third – you are looking for approximately 1 litre stock.

Meanwhile, in a separate saucepan, melt the butter over a low heat and sweat the shallots for a good 10 minutes or so until soft but not coloured. Pour in the reduced pea pod stock and add the podded peas.

Bring up to the boil, then reduce the heat and simmer, uncovered, until the peas are tender – this will take about 5 minutes.

Carefully transfer the soup to a blender and purée until smooth – doing this in batches, if necessary. Return the soup to the pan and reheat gently. Season to taste with salt and freshly ground black pepper.

To make the horseradish cream, in a bowl, mix the crème fraîche with enough horseradish to taste. Season with a little salt and black pepper.

Serve the hot soup in bowls with a piece of smoked trout fillet floating on the surface of each portion. Top each piece of fish with a spoonful of horseradish cream and garnish with a few pea shoots.

**This soup freezes well (without trout fillets, pea shoots and horseradish cream) – freeze for up to 3 months. Defrost thoroughly, then reheat gently until piping hot. See page 8 for more guidance on this. Trout fillets, pea shoots and horseradish cream not suitable for freezing, so simply make the horseradish cream and add the trout fillets and pea shoots garnish just before serving.**

PORK

# Leek and Pancetta Soup with Crisp Parmesan Crumbs

**Slowly braised leeks take on an exceptionally soft and velvety texture in this rich and comforting soup. The Parmesan crumbs add a pleasing crunch as you eat and are so simple to make. They are also really good sprinkled over your favourite pasta dish.**

**Serves 4–6 | Takes 15 minutes to make, 25 minutes to cook**

**For the soup**
**6 leeks, outer leaves trimmed off, washed thoroughly**
**50g unsalted butter**
**1 tbsp olive oil**
**12 slices of pancetta (about 125g), chopped**
**3 cloves garlic, finely sliced**
**2–3 sprigs of fresh thyme**
**200ml white wine**
**1 litre vegetable or chicken stock**
**salt and freshly ground black pepper**

**For the Parmesan crumbs**
**2 tbsp olive oil**
**½ stale ciabatta loaf, torn into rough crumbs**
**2 cloves garlic, crushed**
**2 tbsp finely chopped fresh rosemary leaves**
**3 generous tbsp finely grated fresh Parmesan cheese**

For the soup, slice each leek in half lengthways, then cut on the diagonal into 1cm-thick slices. Melt the butter with the oil in a large, heavy-based saucepan over a low heat. Add the chopped leeks and the pancetta, garlic and thyme sprigs and gently sweat for around 10 minutes or until the leeks are softened. It is really important to cook the leeks over a low heat – unlike onions, caramelised leeks are very bitter so they should never be allowed to take on a colour. A good tip to minimize any risk of this is to wet a scrunched up sheet of greaseproof paper and lay it over the leeks, tucking it in at the edges.

Once the leeks are softened, remove and discard the greaseproof paper, if you are using it. Pour in the wine and simmer until it has evaporated, then add the stock. Bring up to the boil, then lower the heat and simmer gently, uncovered, for about 25 minutes or until the leeks are so soft they are melting. Season to taste with a little salt and plenty of freshly ground black pepper.

Whilst the soup is simmering, make the Parmesan crumbs. Warm the oil in a frying pan over a medium-high heat. Fry the breadcrumbs for a few minutes until they are just starting to turn crisp and golden, stirring occasionally. Stir in the garlic and rosemary and fry for a further minute or two, taking care not to burn the garlic or it will take on a bitter taste. Remove from the heat, stir through the Parmesan cheese and add a generous grind of black pepper. Tip into a serving bowl and set aside.

Remove and discard the thyme sprigs from the soup. Serve the soup in bowls with the Parmesan crumbs passed around separately to sprinkle on as you eat.

**Not suitable for freezing.**

# Chilled Avocado Soup with Garlic Prawns

To me one of the great eating sensations is a contrast between hot and cold and this soup ticks that box in a spectacular way. So simple to make, this chilled creamy avocado soup is topped with hot garlicky prawns and is perfect for a summer evening dinner party.

**Serves 4–6 | Takes 10 minutes to make, plus several hours chilling, 5 minutes to cook**

**For the soup**
**3 ripe avocados, halved, stoned and flesh scooped out**
**1 clove garlic, crushed**
**1 tbsp lemon juice**
**finely grated zest of $\frac{1}{2}$ lemon**
**500ml cold chicken stock (preferably homemade)**
**200ml single cream**
**salt and freshly ground black pepper**

**For the garlic prawns**
**25g unsalted butter**
**300g raw peeled king prawns, butterflied (see Cook's Tip)**
**1 clove garlic, crushed**

For the soup, place the avocado flesh and all the remaining soup ingredients in a blender and purée together until really smooth. Season to taste with salt and freshly ground black pepper. Pour the soup into a bowl, cover and chill very thoroughly in the fridge for several hours before serving.

When you are ready to serve the soup, make the garlic prawns. Melt the butter in a frying pan over a medium-high heat. When it starts to foam, add the prawns and garlic and stir-fry for a few minutes until the prawns are cooked through and pink all over. Season with a little salt and black pepper.

Pour the soup into chilled bowls, scatter with the hot prawns and serve immediately.

**Not suitable for freezing.**

**Cook's Tip**
'Butterflying' prawns simply means partly scoring them through so that they open up during cooking. This not only makes them look really pretty but helps to coat them deep inside with the delicious garlic butter sauce. Simply take each prawn and run a sharp knife down the back, making an incision that goes about halfway through.

# Slow-Cooked Beef Soup with Green Peppers and Sour Cream

**This soup has all the flavours of a rich Hungarian goulash and is a great way of using cheaper cuts of beef like skirt or shin, or even ox cheeks. It is very hearty and warming and makes a great winter lunch for friends.**

**Serves 4–6 | Takes 10 minutes to make, 1–1$\frac{1}{2}$ hours to cook**

2 tbsp olive oil
500g beef for braising (such as skirt, shin or ox cheek), cut into 5–6cm pieces
2 onions, finely sliced
2 green peppers, deseeded and sliced
3 cloves garlic, crushed
800ml beef stock
200ml red wine
2 bay leaves
150ml sour cream
salt and freshly ground black pepper
small bunch of fresh flat-leaf parsley, chopped, to garnish

Heat the oil in a heavy-based saucepan until it is smoking hot. Fry the beef quickly on all sides to sear and caramelise it. Remove the beef to a plate and set aside.

Reduce the heat to medium-high and add the onions and peppers to the pan. Sauté for 5 minutes or until they are starting to soften and take on a little colour at the edges. Stir through the garlic and fry for a further minute. Pour in the stock and wine, add the bay leaves and season with a little salt and freshly ground black pepper.

Return the seared beef to the pan, bring up to the boil, then reduce the heat to a steady simmer. Cover and cook until the beef is so tender it is falling apart – this will take around 1–1$\frac{1}{2}$ hours, depending on the cut of beef you use. If it looks like it is getting too dry, add a splash of cold water.

When the beef is cooked, lift it out on to a plate and shred it using a fork to gently tease it apart.

Stir the sour cream into the soup and warm through, then taste to check the seasoning, adding a little more salt and black pepper, if necessary.

Serve the soup in bowls, with the shredded beef scattered on top. Sprinkle each portion with a little chopped parsley to garnish.

**This soup freezes well (freeze the soup with the cooked, shredded beef stirred through) – freeze for up to 3 months. Defrost thoroughly, then reheat gently until piping hot. See page 8 for more guidance on this.**

# Mussel, Saffron and Cream Soup

**Saffron not only adds a subtle earthy flavour to this creamy seafood soup but it also turns it a gorgeous sunshine-yellow colour. A splash of Pernod makes it extra special, but you can leave this out, if you prefer. This soup should be served with plenty of fresh, crusty French bread.**

**Serves 4–6 | Takes 25 minutes to make, 15–20 minutes to cook**

**1kg fresh mussels (in shell)**
**50g unsalted butter**
**250g shallots, finely chopped**
**5 fresh sage leaves**
**2 sprigs of fresh thyme**
**a sprig of fresh rosemary**
**1 tsp black peppercorns**
**350ml dry white wine**
**2 leeks, washed and finely chopped**
**1 fennel bulb, trimmed and finely chopped**
**1 carrot, finely chopped**
**a generous pinch of saffron strands**
**800ml fish stock**
**2 tbsp cornflour**
**120ml double cream**
**2 tomatoes, skinned, deseeded and finely chopped (see Cook's Tip)**
**2–3 tbsp Pernod (optional)**
**salt and freshly ground black pepper**

Prepare the mussels by washing them thoroughly under cold running water. Pull off any beards and discard any mussels that do not shut firmly when tapped against the edge of the sink. Place the mussels in a bowl and set aside in the fridge.

Melt half of the butter in a large, heavy-based saucepan over a low heat. Add half of the shallots and gently sweat for 5 minutes or until softened but not coloured. Add the herbs, peppercorns and wine and bring up to the boil. Tip in the prepared mussels, cover with a tight-fitting lid and cook over a high heat for 4–5 minutes, shaking the pan from time to time. Once the mussels have opened, use a slotted spoon to lift them into a bowl

and set aside. Strain the cooking liquor through a fine meshed sieve and reserve the liquor.

When the mussels are cool enough to handle, remove most of them from their shells, discarding any that have not opened. Leave 2–3 mussels per person in their shells for the garnish. Keep warm.

Melt the remaining butter in a clean saucepan over a low heat and add the rest of the shallots. Sweat for 5 minutes, before adding the leeks, fennel, carrot and saffron, then continue to cook for another 5 minutes.

Pour in the reserved mussel cooking liquor and bring up to the boil, then reduce the heat and simmer, uncovered, for 5–10 minutes or until the vegetables are tender and the liquid has reduced. Add the stock, bring up to the boil and then simmer steadily for 5 minutes. Remove 2 tablespoons of the liquid and leave it to cool in a small bowl, then stir cornflour paste through the soup and simmer steadily for a further 2–3 minutes or until slightly thickened, stirring.

Stir through the cream, tomatoes and Pernod, if using, and season to taste with salt and freshly ground black pepper. Finally, add the shelled mussels and allow them to warm through for a minute or so before serving. Serve the hot soup in bowls, garnished with the reserved mussels in their shells.

**Not suitable for freezing.**
.

CHICKEN

# Chicken and Asparagus Soup with Tarragon

This is not the quickest of recipes in this book, but boy is it worth the time spent making it. I love tarragon whose mild aniseed flavour is the perfect partner to anything creamy, and it works really well in this rich soup.

**Serves 4–6 | Takes 1¼ hours to make, 20 minutes to cook**

**For the stock**
**4 chicken thighs, bone-in, skin removed**
**1 carrot, roughly chopped**
**1 stick celery, roughly chopped**
**1 onion, unpeeled and quartered**
**1 bay leaf**
**2 sprigs of fresh thyme**
**a few fresh parsley stalks**
**1 tsp black peppercorns**

**For the soup**
**50g unsalted butter**
**1 leek, washed and finely chopped**
**1 clove garlic, crushed**
**175ml white wine**
**300g asparagus (woody ends trimmed off), sliced diagonally into 2cm lengths**
**150ml double cream**
**a few sprigs of fresh tarragon, leaves finely chopped**
**salt and freshly ground black pepper**

Put all the stock ingredients into a large saucepan and cover with 1.2 litres cold water. Bring up to the boil, then reduce the heat to the minimum, cover with a tight-fitting lid and simmer very gently for 50–60 minutes or until the chicken is tender and coming away from the bone.

Using a slotted spoon, lift out the chicken and set aside on a plate to cool a little. Strain the stock, reserving the liquid to make the base of the soup. Discard the vegetables and herbs.

For the soup, melt the butter in a clean saucepan over a low heat and gently sweat the leek for around 10 minutes or until soft and translucent – cook the leek slowly so as not to burn it or it will impart a bitter note that will spoil your soup. Add the garlic and fry for a further minute, before pouring in the wine. Turn up the heat a little and simmer for a few minutes or until the wine has reduced.

Add the reserved stock and season with a little salt and freshly ground black pepper. Bring up to the boil, then reduce the heat and simmer, uncovered, for 10 minutes.

Stir through the asparagus and simmer, uncovered, for a further 5 minutes or until the asparagus is tender but still with a little bite.

Whilst the soup is simmering, remove the chicken meat from the bones and cut it into bite-sized pieces. Add to the soup, along with the cream and tarragon and warm through gently for 5 minutes or so.

Taste to check the seasoning, adding a little more salt and black pepper, if necessary. Serve immediately in bowls.

**Not suitable for freezing.**

# Clam, Parsley and Lemon Soup

**I love clams, particularly the surf clams that taste so sweet when they are in season in the autumn and winter. The inspiration for this soup is one of my all-time favourite pasta dishes, spaghetti alle vongole, where clams are steamed in white wine and tossed in olive oil, parsley and a touch of chilli. Delicious.**

**Serves 4–6 | Takes 15 minutes to make, 15 minutes to cook**

1.5kg fresh clams (in shell)
175ml white wine
3 tbsp olive oil
1 onion, finely chopped
1 carrot, finely chopped
1 stick celery, finely chopped
3 cloves garlic, finely sliced
2 sprigs of fresh rosemary
2 wide strips of pared lemon peel
a pinch of dried chilli flakes
   (optional)
4 tomatoes, skinned, deseeded
   and chopped
2 potatoes, cut into 1cm dice
1 litre fish stock
generous handful of fresh flat-leaf
   parsley, roughly chopped
salt and freshly ground black
   pepper
extra virgin olive oil, for drizzling
1 lemon, cut into wedges, to serve

Wash the clams thoroughly under cold running water and discard any clams that do not shut firmly when tapped against the edge of the sink. Place the clams in a large saucepan. Pour over the wine and bring up to the boil, then cover and cook for 5 minutes, shaking the pan once or twice. Once the clams are cooked and have opened, strain them through a fine mesh sieve and reserve the cooking liquor.

When the clams are cool enough to handle, remove two-thirds of them from their shells, discarding any that have not opened. Leave the rest in their shells for the garnish. Set all the clams, shelled and unshelled, aside and keep warm whilst you get on with the soup.

Heat the olive oil in a heavy-based saucepan and gently fry the onion for 5 minutes or until it starts to soften. Add the carrot, celery and garlic, along with the rosemary sprigs, lemon peel and chilli flakes, if using, and sweat for a further 5 minutes.

Stir through the tomatoes and potatoes and pour over the stock. Bring up to the boil, then reduce the heat and simmer for 10 minutes or so until the potatoes are just tender. Fish out and discard the rosemary and lemon peel.

Add the shelled cooked clams and warm them through for a minute or two. Remove the pan from the heat, stir in the chopped parsley and season to taste with salt and freshly ground black pepper.

Serve the hot soup in bowls, garnished with the reserved clams in their shells and drizzled with a little extra virgin olive oil, with lemon wedges to squeeze over as you eat.

**Not suitable for freezing.**

# Prawn and Basil Bisque

As this elegant soup is quite special and worthy of any dinner party table, I would recommend saving it for an occasion when you have time to make your own fish stock. Don't be tempted to slice up the basil until just before you serve it, otherwise it with lose both its colour and pungency over time.

**Serves 4–6 | Takes 35 minutes to make, about 20 minutes to cook**

**600g raw shell-on king prawns**
**4 tbsp olive oil**
**1 litre fish stock (preferably homemade – see page 56)**
**200g shallots, very finely chopped**
**2 carrots, finely chopped**
**2 cloves garlic, each crushed separately**
**150ml white vermouth (such as Noilly Prat)**
**1 tbsp tomato purée**
**a pinch of cayenne pepper (optional)**
**generous handful of fresh basil leaves**
**25g unsalted butter**
**salt and freshly ground black pepper**
**a little double cream and a few fresh basil leaves, to garnish**

Reserve a couple of prawns per person (total of 8–12) as a garnish and set aside.

Peel the rest of the prawns, placing the peeled prawns on to a plate and adding all the shells, including the heads, to a large saucepan. Add 1 tablespoon of oil to the pan and toss well to coat the shells and heads all over. Fry over a medium-high heat for 5 minutes or until they are pink all over and just starting to colour a little at the edges.

Pour in the stock and bring up to the boil, then reduce the heat and simmer, uncovered, for 15 minutes. Strain, reserving the prawn-infused stock and discarding the prawn shells and heads.

Whilst the stock is simmering, finely chop the peeled prawns and set aside.

Pour the rest of the oil into a clean saucepan and sweat the shallots and carrots over a very low heat for a good 10 minutes or so until they are very soft, but without letting them colour.

Add 1 of the crushed cloves of garlic and fry for a further minute or two, before pouring in the vermouth. Let it bubble and reduce for 5 minutes, before pouring over the strained stock. Stir through the tomato purée and cayenne pepper, if using, and season with a little salt and freshly ground black pepper.

Bring up to the boil, then reduce the heat and simmer until the shallots and carrots are soft to the point of collapse – this should take 10–15 minutes. Add the chopped prawns and cook for a further 3 minutes.

Carefully transfer the soup to a blender and purée until smooth – doing this in batches, if necessary. Return the soup to the pan and reheat gently, then taste to check the seasoning, adding a little more salt and black pepper, if necessary. Chop the handful of basil leaves into fine strips and stir through the soup just before serving.

When you are ready to serve the soup, prepare the prawn garnish. Melt the butter in a small frying pan over a medium heat. When it is foaming, add the reserved whole prawns and the remaining garlic and stir-fry for a few minutes or until the prawns are cooked through and pink all over.

Serve the soup immediately in bowls with a little cream swirled on top of each portion. Garnish with the garlic prawns and a few basil leaves.

**This soup is best made fresh, so is not suitable for freezing.**

# Cream of Scallop Soup with Crisp Smoked Bacon

**This soup is really rich and creamy with a delicate seafood taste. I love the crunchy bacon sprinkles that add a fantastic contrasting texture as you eat – scallops and bacon are made for each other.**

**Serves 4–6 |Takes 10–15 minutes to make, 15–20 minutes to cook**

**400g fresh scallops (shelled weight)**
**50g unsalted butter**
**1 onion, very finely chopped**
**2 bay leaves**
**400g potatoes, cut into 1cm dice**
**600ml fish stock**
**175ml white wine**
**200ml double cream**
**1 tbsp olive oil**
**200g smoked bacon lardons**
**salt and freshly ground black pepper**

Reserve 1 whole scallop per person for the garnish, then chop the remaining scallops into 1cm dice. Set aside.

Melt the butter in a large, heavy-based saucepan and gently sweat the onion for around 10 minutes or until soft and translucent. Add the bay leaves and potatoes, then pour over the stock and wine. Bring up to the boil, then lower the heat and simmer, uncovered, for 10–15 minutes or until the potatoes are falling apart. Remove and discard the bay leaves.

Carefully transfer the soup to a blender and purée until really smooth, then return to the pan. Stir in the cream, then bring the soup back up to a simmer. Add the chopped scallop meat and simmer for 2–3 minutes. Season to taste with a little salt and plenty of freshly ground black pepper. Keep warm whilst you prepare the bacon garnish.

Heat the oil in a small frying pan over a medium-high heat. Add the bacon lardons and fry for a few minutes or until crisp and golden. Remove and drain on kitchen paper. With the heat high, quickly sear the reserved whole scallops in the same pan for a minute or so on each side, so they are cooked through with a little colour on the outside.

Serve the hot soup in bowls and garnish each portion with a seared scallop and a sprinkling of crisp bacon.

**Not suitable for freezing.**

# Roast Red Pepper Soup with Garlic and Basil Cream

**Thanks to the long, gentle roasting of the peppers, this sweet and summery soup has an amazing velvety texture. A creamy, yet pungent basil dressing is swirled over at the last minute to bring your senses alive as you eat.**

**Serves 4–6 | Takes 50 minutes to make, 10 minutes to cook**

**For the soup**
**8 red peppers**
**50g unsalted butter**
**6 shallots, finely chopped**
**1 litre vegetable stock**

**For the garlic and basil cream**
**generous bunch of fresh basil, leaves only**
**2 cloves garlic, chopped**
**150ml double cream**
**salt and freshly ground black pepper**

Preheat the oven to 160°C/gas 3.

Start the soup. Place the red peppers, whole and unpeeled, in a roasting tin and cook in the oven for around 40 minutes or until they are soft and collapsing.

Whilst the peppers are roasting, make the garlic and basil cream. Purée the basil leaves and garlic with the cream, either in a mini food processor or using a stick blender in a bowl. Season to taste with salt and freshly ground black pepper and set aside at room temperature to allow the flavours to mingle.

Continue with the soup. Melt the butter in a heavy-based saucepan over a low heat, then sweat the shallots for 10 minutes or until they are translucent. Take care not to cook them over too high a heat – you are trying to turn them into a softly melting mass rather than caramelise them.

When the peppers are done, remove them from the oven and let them cool a little so you can handle them. Slice them open and carefully remove and discard all the seeds, white membranes and stalks. Roughly chop the flesh and add to the shallots in the pan. Pour in the stock, then bring up to a steady simmer and cook, uncovered, for 5 minutes.

Carefully transfer the soup to a blender and purée until completely smooth. Pass the soup through a sieve back into the pan and reheat gently until hot, then taste to check the seasoning, adding salt and black pepper, if necessary.

Serve the soup hot in bowls, with the basil cream swirled over the top. This soup is also good served cold on a hot summers day – just make sure it is really thoroughly chilled, rather than lukewarm, before serving.

**This soup freezes well, but the garlic and basil cream is best made fresh as it will loose its herbal pungency. Freeze the soup for up to 3 months. Defrost thoroughly, then reheat gently until piping hot. See page 8 for more guidance on this. Garlic and basil cream not suitable for freezing, so simply make this fresh before serving.**

# Creamy Aubergine Soup with Walnut, Parsley and Pomegranate Salsa

The lovely creamy aubergine dip, baba ganoush, from the Middle East inspired me to make this soup. The crunchy salsa on top contains pomegranate molasses, a wonderful sweet but sharp syrup made from the juice of the fruit. It has a fantastically unusual flavour that is great in all sorts of salad dressings. You can find it in Arabic grocers or sometimes in the special ingredients section of some supermarkets.

**Serves 4–6 | Takes 45 minutes to make, 10 minutes to cook**

**For the soup**
**4 medium aubergines**
**6 tbsp olive oil**
**4 onions, finely chopped**
**4 cloves garlic, crushed**
**2 tbsp sesame seeds**
**1 litre vegetable stock**
**lemon juice, or to taste**
**salt and freshly ground black**
**   pepper**

**For the salsa**
**60g walnut halves**
**seeds from $\frac{1}{2}$ a large**
**   pomegranate**
**small bunch of fresh flat-leaf**
**   parsley, chopped**
**1 tbsp extra virgin olive oil**
**1–2 tsp pomegranate molasses, or**
**   to taste**

Preheat the oven to 180°C/gas 4.

Make the soup. Prick the aubergines all over with a fork, place them on a baking tray and roast in the oven for around 45 minutes or until they are completely soft and collapsing. Remove the aubergines from the oven, cut them in half lengthways and carefully scoop out the flesh with a spoon (it will be hot!), then roughly chop it.

Whilst the aubergines are cooking, heat the olive oil in a large, heavy-based saucepan over a low heat and fry the onions very slowly until they are meltingly soft. Don't rush this step, you don't want to really add any colour to the onions, so cook them as gently as possible for at least 30 minutes.

Add half of the crushed garlic and the sesame seeds and fry for a further minute. Stir through the chopped aubergine and pour in the stock. Bring up to the boil, then reduce the heat and simmer, uncovered, for 5 minutes.

Carefully transfer the soup to a blender and purée until completely smooth, then return to the pan and reheat gently. Season to taste with a little salt and freshly ground black pepper. Stir through the remaining crushed garlic and add a squeeze of lemon juice to taste.

Meanwhile, to make the salsa, dry-fry the walnuts in a small frying pan for just a minute or two. As soon as you smell a nutty aroma wafting up from the pan, remove from the heat, tip them on to a chopping board and roughly chop. Transfer the chopped walnuts to a small bowl and add the pomegranate seeds and chopped parsley. Stir through the extra virgin olive oil and pomegranate molasses and season with a little salt and black pepper.

Serve the hot soup in bowls, sprinkled with a little of the salsa. Serve the remaining salsa in a bowl on the side to add extra as you eat.

**Not suitable for freezing.**

**157 SOUP! INDEX**

British and American cookbooks use different measuring systems. In the UK, dry ingredients are measured by weight, with the metric system increasingly replacing the Imperial one, while in the US they are measured by volume.

# Weight

| | | | |
|---|---|---|---|
| **7g** | ¼ ounce | **200g** | 7 ounces |
| **20g** | ¾ ounce | **220–225g** | 8 ounces |
| **25–30g** | 1 ounce | **250–260g** | 9 ounces |
| **40g** | 1½ ounces | **300g** | 10½ ounces |
| **50g** | 1¾ ounces | **325g** | 11½ ounces |
| **60–65g** | 2¼ ounces | **350g** | 12 ounces |
| **70–75g** | 2½ ounces | **400g** | 14 ounces |
| **80g** | 2¾ ounces | **450g** | 1 pound |
| **90g** | 3¼ ounces | **500g** | 1 pound 2 ounces |
| **100g** | 3½ ounces | **600g** | 1 pound 5 ounces |
| **110–115g** | 4 ounces | **700g** | 1 pound 9 ounces |
| **120–130g** | 4½ ounces | **750g** | 1 pound 10 ounces |
| **140g** | 5 ounces | **800g** | 1¾ pounds |
| **150g** | 5½ ounces | **900g** | 2 pounds |
| **175–180g** | 6 ounces | **1kg** | 2¼ pounds |

# Volume

| | | | |
|---|---|---|---|
| **50ml** | 1¾ fl oz | **300ml** | 10 fl oz |
| **60ml** | 2 fl oz (4 tablespoons/¼ cup) | **350ml** | 12 fl oz |
| **75ml** | 2½ fl oz (5 tablespoons) | **400ml** | 14 fl oz |
| **90ml** | 3 fl oz (⅜ cup) | **450ml** | 15 fl oz |
| **100ml** | 3½ fl oz | **475ml** | 16 fl oz (2 cups) |
| **125ml** | 4 fl oz (½ cup) | **500ml** | 18 fl oz |
| **150ml** | 5 fl oz (⅔ cup) | **600ml** | 20 fl oz |
| **175ml** | 6 fl oz | **800ml** | 28 fl oz |
| **200ml** | 7 fl oz | **850ml** | 30 fl oz |
| **250ml** | 8 fl oz (1 cup) | **1 litre** | 35 fl oz (4 cups) |

# Length

| | | | |
|---|---|---|---|
| **5mm** | ¼ inch | **8cm** | 3¼ inches |
| **1cm** | ½ inch | **9cm** | 3½ inches |
| **2cm** | ¾ inch | **10cm** | 4 inches |
| **2.5cm** | 1 inch | **12cm** | 4½ inches |
| **3cm** | 1¼ inches | **14cm** | 5½ inches |
| **4cm** | 1½ inches | **20cm** | 8 inches |
| **5cm** | 2 inches | **24cm** | 9½ inches |
| **6cm** | 2½ inches | **30cm** | 12 inches |